**W9-BXT-574**

Exit,
Voice,
and
Loyalty

# Exit,
# Voice,
# and
# Loyalty

Responses to Decline
in Firms, Organizations,
and States

## Albert O. Hirschman

Harvard University Press
Cambridge, Massachusetts
and London, England

Library of Congress Catalog Card Number: 77-99517
ISBN 0-674-27660-4
Printed in the United States of America

To Eugenio Colorni (1909–1944),
who taught me about small ideas
and how they may grow

# Preface

This is an unpremeditated book. It has its origin in an observation on rail transport in Nigeria which occupied a paragraph in my previous book, reproduced here at the start of Chapter 4. One critic objected to that paragraph because, as he charitably expressed himself, "there must be a lot of assumptions hidden there somewhere." After a while I decided to pursue these assumptions into their hiding places and was soon off on an absorbing expedition which lasted the full year that I had planned to spend in leisurely meditation at the Center for Advanced Study in the Behavioral Sciences.

The principal reason for which I persevered will be obvious to the reader: I had come upon a manner of analyzing certain economic processes which promised to illuminate a wide range of social, political, and indeed moral phenomena. But this book does not use the tools of one discipline for the purpose of annexing another. As is shown particularly in the appendixes, the concepts I develop can be translated into the language of traditional economic analysis, and may possibly enrich it; but by no means do they uniquely belong there. I rather became concerned that the concepts of "exit" and "voice" might be too broad as my writing expanded with surprising ease into ever new territories. The principal concession I made to these worries was to keep this book short. Otherwise, having found my own unifying way of looking at issues as diverse as competition and the two-party system, divorce and the American character, black power and the failure of "unhappy" top officials to resign over Vietnam, I decided to let myself go a little.

The Center provided a particularly favorable environment for this sort of project. I made ample use of the "right to buttonhole" the other Fellows which is, I believe, an essential part of the oral tradition at the Center. My intellectual debts to those who spent the year with me are generally acknowledged in footnote references. Special gratitude is owed to Gabriel Almond who contributed important critical points while being permanently supportive of my enterprise; to a comment by Richard Lowenthal that led me to write Chapter 6; and to Tjalling Koopmans who helped sharpen some of the technical arguments, as did Robert Wilson of the Stanford Business School.

The finished manuscript was read by Abram Bergson and Albert Fishlow who both made a number of incisive comments and suggestions. At an earlier stage, I derived considerable benefit from seminars at Harvard, Yale, and Boston College where I discussed some of my ideas. In the course of 1967, David S. French searched for precursors to them in the vast literature on competition, fortunately without much success.

It was gratifying that Philip G. Zimbardo, professor of psychology at Stanford University, found some of my hypotheses of sufficient interest to plan for an experimental verification. The proposed research is described in an appendix.

Hildegarde Teilhet typed and retyped the manuscript with zest and skill.

My wife, who contributed so much to my previous books, wisely decided she would make me enjoy the California sunshine vicariously.

Stanford, California
July 1969

A.O.H.

# Contents

Contents

Exit,
Voice,
and
Loyalty

# 1
# Introduction
# and Doctrinal Background

Under any economic, social, or political system, individuals, business firms, and organizations in general are subject to lapses from efficient, rational, law-abiding, virtuous, or otherwise functional behavior. No matter how well a society's basic institutions are devised, failures of some actors to live up to the behavior which is expected of them are bound to occur, if only for all kinds of accidental reasons. Each society learns to live with a certain amount of such dysfunctional or mis-behavior; but lest the misbehavior feed on itself and lead to general decay, society must be able to marshal from within itself forces which will make as many of the faltering actors as possible revert to the behavior required for its proper functioning. This book undertakes initially a reconnaissance of these forces as they operate in the economy; the concepts to be developed will, however, be found to be applicable not only to economic operators such as business firms, but to a wide variety of noneconomic organizations and situations.

While moralists and political scientists have been much concerned with rescuing individuals from immoral behavior, societies from corruption, and governments from decay, economists have paid little attention to *repairable lapses* of economic actors. There are two reasons for this neglect. First, in economics one assumes either fully and undeviatingly rational behavior or, at the very least, an *unchanging level* of rationality on the part of the economic actors. Deterioration of a firm's performance may result from an adverse shift in supply and demand conditions while the willingness and ability of the firm to maximize profits (or growth rate or whatever) are unimpaired; but it could also reflect some "loss of maximizing aptitude or energy" with supply and demand factors being un-

1

changed. The latter interpretation would immediately raise the question how the firm's maximizing energy can be brought back up to par. But the usual interpretation is the former one; and in that case, the reversibility of changes in objective supply and demand conditions is much more in doubt. In other words, economists have typically assumed that a firm that falls behind (or gets ahead) does so *"for a good reason"*; the concept—central to this book—of a random and more or less easily "repairable lapse" has been alien to their reasoning.

The second cause of the economist's unconcern about lapses is related to the first. In the traditional model of the competitive economy, recovery from any lapse is not really essential. As one firm loses out in the competitive struggle, its market share is taken up and its factors are hired by others, including newcomers; in the upshot, total resources may well be better allocated. With this picture in mind, the economist can afford to watch lapses of any one of *his* patients (such as business firms) with far greater equanimity than either the moralist who is convinced of the intrinsic worth of every one of *his* patients (individuals) or the political scientist whose patient (the state) is unique and irreplaceable.

Having accounted for the economist's unconcern we can immediately question its justification: for the image of the economy as a fully competitive system where changes in the fortunes of individual firms are exclusively caused by basic shifts of comparative advantage is surely a defective representation of the real world. In the first place, there are the well-known, large realms of monopoly, oligopoly, and monopolistic competition: deterioration in performance of firms operating in that part of the economy could result in more or less permanent *pockets* of inefficiency and neglect; it must obviously be viewed with an alarm approaching that of the political scientist who sees his polity's integrity being threatened by strife, corruption, or boredom. But even where vigorous competition prevails, unconcern with the possibility of restoring temporarily laggard firms to vigor is hardly justified. Precisely in sectors where there are large numbers of firms competing with one another in similar conditions, declines in the fortunes of individual firms are just as likely to be due to random, subjective factors that are reversible or remediable as to permanent adverse shifts in cost and demand conditions. In these circumstances, mechanisms of recuperation would play a most useful role in avoiding social losses as well as human hardship.

At this point, it will be interjected that such a mechanism of recuperation is readily available through competition itself. Is not competition supposed to keep a firm "on its toes"? And if the firm has already slipped, isn't it the experience of declining revenue and the threat of extinction through competition that will cause its managers to make a major effort to bring performance back up to where it should be?

There can be no doubt that competition is one major mechanism of recuperation. It will here be argued, however (1) that the implications of this particular function of competition have not been adequately spelled out and (2) that a major alternative mechanism can come into play either when the competitive mechanism is unavailable or as a complement to it.

## Enter "Exit" and "Voice"

The argument to be presented starts with the firm producing saleable outputs for customers; but it will be found to be largely—and, at times, principally—applicable to organizations (such as voluntary associations, trade unions, or political parties) that provide services to their members without direct monetary counterpart. The performance of a firm or an organization is assumed to be subject to deterioration for unspecified, random causes which are neither so compelling nor so durable as to prevent a return to previous performance levels, provided managers direct their attention and energy to that task. The deterioration in performance is reflected most typically and generally, that is, for both firms and other organizations, in an absolute or comparative deterioration of the *quality* of the product or service provided.[1] Management then finds out about its failings via two alternative routes:

(1) Some customers stop buying the firm's products or some members leave the organization: this is the *exit option*. As a result, revenues drop, membership declines, and management is impelled to search for ways and means to correct whatever faults have led to exit.

(2) The firm's customers or the organization's members express their dissatisfaction directly to management or to some other authority to which management is subordinate or through general protest addressed to anyone who cares to listen: this is the *voice option*. As a result, management once again engages in a search for the causes and possible cures of customers' and members' dissatisfaction.

The remainder of this book is largely devoted to the

1. For business firms operating in situations of monopoly or monopolistic competition, performance deterioriation can also be reflected in cost and resulting price increases or in a combination of quality drops and price increases. On the other hand, changes in either price or quality are ruled out when both are rigidly dictated by a perfectly competitive market; in this admittedly unrealistic situation, deterioration can manifest itself only via increases in cost which, with price and quality unchanged, will lead straightaway to a decline in net revenue. Under perfect competition, then, managers learn about their failings directly and exclusively from financial evidence generated within the firm, without any intermediation on the part of the customers who remain totally unaware of the firm's troubles. It is perhaps because the whole range of phenomena here described has no place in the perfectly competitive model that it has not been paid attention to by economists.

comparative analysis of these two options and to their interplay. I will investigate questions such as: Under what conditions will the exit option prevail over the voice option and vice versa? What is the comparative efficiency of the two options as mechanisms of recuperation? In what situations do both options come into play jointly? What institutions could serve to perfect each of the two options as mechanisms of recuperation? Are institutions perfecting the exit option compatible with those designed to improve the working of the voice option?

## Latitude for Deterioration, and Slack in Economic Thought

Before setting out to answer some of these questions, I shall now step back briefly and indicate how I conceive the subject of this book to be related to economic and social science thought around us.

Talking with students of animal behavior (at the Center for Advanced Study in the Behavioral Sciences) about the social organization of primates I learnt about the smoothness and efficiency with which leadership succession, a problem human societies have found so intractable, was handled in certain baboon bands. Here is how the process is described for a typical band of Hamadryas baboons lorded over by one male leader:

Sub-adult males steal very young females from their mothers and attend them with every semblance of solicitous maternal care. The young female is rigorously controlled, and repeated retrieval trains her not to go away . . . At this stage there is no sexual behaviour, the female being yet two to three years from child bearing . . . As these young interlopers mature and the overlord ages, the younger animal starts initiating group movements although the direction of eventual movement is dependent upon the older animal's choice. A highly complex relationship develops between the two animals which, by paying close attention to one another and by reciprocal "notification," cooperate in governing group movement. Old males retain command of group direction but gradually relinquish sexual control over their females to the younger male animal . . . It seems that eventually old males resign entirely from their original reproduction units but retain great influence within the band as a whole, and young males refer to them continuously particularly before developing the direction of march.[2]

Compare this marvel of gradualness and continuity with the violent ups and downs to which human societies have always been subject as "bad" government followed upon "good," and as strong or wise or good leaders were succeeded by weaklings, fools, or criminals.

The reason for which humans have failed to develop a finely built social process assuring continuity and steady quality in leadership is probably that they did not have to. Most human societies are marked by the existence of a surplus above subsistence. The counterpart of this surplus is society's ability to take considerable deterioration in its stride. A lower level of performance, which would mean disaster for baboons, merely causes discomfort, at least initially, to humans.

The wide latitude human societies have for deterioration is the inevitable counterpart of man's increasing productivity and control over his environment. Occasional decline as well as prolonged mediocrity—in relation to achievable performance levels—must be counted among the many penalties of progress. A priori it would seem futile, therefore, to look for social arrangements that

2. John Hurrell Crook, "The Socio-Ecology of Primates," in J. H. Crook, ed., *Social Behaviour in Animals and Man* (to be published by Academic Press, London). The passage quoted summarizes research by Hans Kummer, "Social Organization of Hamadryas Baboons," *Bibliotheca Primatologica*, no. 6 (Basle: S. Karger, 1968).

would wholly eliminate any sort of deterioration of polities and of their various constituent entities. Because of the surplus and the resulting latitude, any homeostatic controls with which human societies might be equipped are bound to be rough.

Recognition of this unpleasant truth has been impeded by a recurring utopian dream: that economic progress, while increasing the surplus above subsistence, will also bring with it disciplines and sanctions of such severity as to rule out any backsliding that may be due, for example, to faulty political processes. In the eighteenth century the expansion of commerce and of industry was sometimes hailed not so much because of the increase in well-being that it would make possible, but because it would bring with it powerful restraints on the willfulness of the prince and thereby reduce and perhaps eliminate the system's latitude for deterioration. One characteristic passage from Sir James Steuart's *Inquiry into the Principles of Political Oeconomy* (1767) will suffice to make the point:

How hurtful soever the natural and immediate effects of political revolutions may have been formerly, when the mechanism of government was more simple than at present, they are now brought under such restrictions, by the complicated system of modern oeconomy, that the evil which might otherwise result from them may be guarded against with ease . . .

The power of a modern prince, let it be by the constitution of his kingdom ever so absolute, immediately becomes limited so soon as he establishes the plan of oeconomy . . . If his authority formerly resembled the solidity and force of the wedge (which may indifferently be made use of, for splitting of timber, stones and other hard bodies, and which may be thrown aside and taken up again at pleasure), it will at length come to resemble the delicacy of the watch, which is good for no other purpose than to mark the progression of time, and which is immediately destroyed, if put to any other use, or touched with any but the gentlest hand . . . modern oeconomy, therefore, is the most effectual bridle ever was invented against the folly of despotism.[3]

This noble hope echoes nearly two hundred years later in the writings of a Latin American intellectual similarly predicting, against all likelihood, that economic progress and latitude for deterioration will be negatively, rather than positively, correlated:

[In the pre-coffee era, policy makers] are lyrical and romantic because they cannot yet defer to a product whose output is constantly on the increase. It is a time of childhood and play. Coffee will bring maturity and seriousness. It will not permit Colombians to continue playing fast and loose with the national economy. The ideological absolutism will disappear and the epoch of moderation and sobriety will dawn . . . Coffee is incompatible with anarchy.[4]

History has cruelly disappointed the expectations of both Sir James Steuart and Nieto Arteta that economic growth and technical progress would erect secure barriers against "despotism," "anarchy," and irresponsible behavior in general. Yet their line of thought is hardly extinct. It is, in fact, not unrelated to today's widespread belief that a major war is unthinkable and therefore impossible in the nuclear age.

The common assumption of these constructs is simply stated: while technical progress increases society's surplus above subsistence it also introduces a mechanism of the utmost complexity and delicacy, so that certain types of social misbehavior which previously had unfortunate

3. (Chicago: University of Chicago Press, 1966), I, 277, 278–279.
4. Luis Eduardo Nieto Arteta, *El café en la sociedad colombiana* (Bogotá: Breviarios de orientación colombiana, 1958), pp. 34–35. This posthumously published essay was written in 1947, only a year before the outbreak of the sanguinary civil disturbances known as *la violencia*, just as Sir James Steuart wrote about the definitive conquest of despotism not long before the rise of Napoleon.

but tolerable consequences would now be so clearly disastrous that they will be more securely barred than before.

As a result society is, and then again it is not, in a surplus situation: it is producing a surplus, but is not at liberty *not* to produce it or to produce less of it than is possible; in effect, social behavior is as simply and as rigidly prescribed and constrained as it is in a no-surplus, bare subsistence situation.

The economist cannot fail to note the similarity of the situation with the model of perfect competition. For this model contains the same basic paradox: society as a whole produces a comfortable and perhaps steadily increasing surplus, but every individual firm considered in isolation is barely getting by, so that a single false step will be its undoing. As a result, everyone is constantly made to perform at the top of his form and society as a whole is operating on its—forever expanding—"production frontier," with economically useful resources fully occupied. This image of a relentlessly *taut economy* has held a privileged place in economic analysis, even when perfect competition was recognized as a purely theoretical construct with little reality-content.

These various observations add up to a syndrome, namely, to man's fundamentally ambivalent attitude toward his ability to produce a surplus: he likes surplus but is fearful of paying its price. While unwilling to give up progress he hankers after the simple rigid constraints on behavior that governed him when he, like all other creatures, was totally absorbed by the need to satisfy his most basic drives. Who knows but that this hankering is at the root of the paradise myth! It seems plausible, indeed, that the *rise* of man above the narrowly constrained condition of all other living creatures was frequently sensed, though it can hardly ever have been avowed, as a *fall;* and a radical but basically simple act of the imagination may well have metamorphosed this condition which one was really yearning for into its exact opposite, the Garden of Eden.[5]

But we must leave paradise and return to social thought, for there is another side to our story. The simple idea that the ability to produce a surplus above subsistence makes it possible and indeed likely that occasionally less than the maximum producible surplus will be produced has not gone wholly unnoticed. In fact, next to the traditional model of the permanently *taut* economy, elements of a theory of the *slack* economy begin to be available. I am not referring now to unemployment and depression economics —the slack associated with these phenomena results from malfunctions at the macroeconomic level which frustrate firms and individuals in their supposedly undiminished zeal to maximize profits and satisfaction. Nor is the question of slack involved in the dispute about what it is that business firms, and particularly the large corporations, really do maximize: profits, growth, market shares, community goodwill, or some composite functions of such objectives. The assumption underlying this dispute is that, whatever it is that firms do, they do it the best they can even though the criterion for "best" performance is becoming rather murky. Finally I am not concerned with the large body of writings showing that the actions of conscientiously maximizing private producers and consumers may fail to produce a *social* optimum, because of the existence of monopolistic elements and externalities.

5. Samuel Johnson intimated this thought in his fable about the Happy Valley of Abyssinia. When Prince Rasselas first analyzes the discontent he feels in the paradiselike valley, he compares his condition to that of some grazing goats in the following terms: "What makes the difference between man and all the rest of the animal creation? Every beast that strays beside me has the same corporal necessities with myself; he is hungry and crops the grass, he is thirsty and drinks the stream, his thirst and hunger are appeased, he is satisfied and sleeps; he rises again and is hungry, he is again fed and is at rest. I am hungry or thirsty like him, but when thirst or hunger cease, I am not at rest; I am like him pained with want, but am not, like him, satisfied with fulness." (Samuel Johnson, *Rasselas*, II.)

Here again the difference between actual and potential output is not due to some "failure of nerve" at the microeconomic level. But of late there has been increasing attention to the possibility of just such a failure.

A seminal contribution in this area was H. A. Simon's suggestion that firms are normally aiming at no more than a "satisfactory" rather than at the highest possible rate of profits.[6] This notion was given considerable underpinning in 1963 by Richard Cyert and James March, who in their book *A Behavioral Theory of the Firm*[7] introduced the concept of "organizational slack." At about the same time, Gary Becker showed that some of the basic and empirically well-tested microeconomic theorems (for example, that market demand curves for individual commodities are negatively inclined) are consistent with a wide range of irrational and inefficient behavior on the part of consumers and producers even though these theorems had originally been derived on the assumption of undeviating rationality.[8] The importance of slack was later affirmed in a particularly sweeping form by Harvey Leibenstein.[9] Finally, in a widely discussed polemical essay, Professor M. M. Postan has recently contended that Britain's economic ailments are better understood by focusing on microeconomic slack than on any mistaken macroeconomic policies. He writes:

6. H. A. Simon, "A Behavioral Model of Rational Choice," *Quarterly Journal of Economics*, 69:98–118 (1952). An early, completely forgotten empirical work with a related theme has the significant title *The Triumph of Mediocrity in Business*, by Horace Secrist, published in 1933 by the Bureau of Business Research, Northwestern University. The book contains an elaborate statistical demonstration that, over a period of time, initially high-performing firms will on the average show deterioration while the initial low performers will exhibit improvement.

7. Richard M. Cyert and James G. March, *Behavioral Theory of the Firm* (Englewood Cliffs, N.J.: Prentice-Hall, Inc., 1963).

8. Gary S. Becker, "Irrational Behavior and Economic Theory," *Journal of Political Economy*, 52:1–13 (February 1962).

9. Harvey Leibenstein, "Allocative Efficiency versus X-Efficiency," *American Economic Review*, 56:392–415 (June 1966).

For many (perhaps most) of these . . . ailments the morbid causes will be found not in the malfunctioning of the life processes in the body economic, such as the low rate of savings, or the high level of prices, or the insufficient allocation of national resources to research and development, but in specific failures of its individual cells—management, design, salesmanship, or the behavior of groups of labor.[10]

I feel considerable kinship with this group of writings for I had adopted a similar position in dealing with the problem of development. The basic proposition of *The Strategy of Economic Development* (1958) was that "development depends not so much on finding optimal combinations for given resources and factors of production as on calling forth and enlisting for development purposes resources and abilities that are hidden, scattered or badly utilized." [11] And the term slack actually came under my pen when I summarized later on the essential argument of that book in an article co-authored with C. E. Lindblom:

At any one point of time, an economy's resources are not to be considered as rigidly fixed in amount, and more resources or factors of production will come into play if development is marked by sectoral imbalances that galvanize private entrepreneurs or public authorities into action . . . The crucial, but plausible, assumption here is that there is some "slack" in the economy; and that additional investment, hours of work, productivity, and decision making can be squeezed out of it by pressure mechanisms.[12]

Various reasons have been invoked for explaining slack. Leibenstein's emphasis is on the uncertainties surrounding the production function and on the nonmarketability

10. M. M. Postan, "A Plague of Economists?" *Encounter* (January 1968), p. 44.

11. (New Haven: Yale University Press, 1958), p. 5.

12. "Economic Development, Research and Development, Policy Making: Some Converging Views," *Behavioral Science*, 7:211–212 (April 1962).

of managerial and other skills. Cyert and March refer primarily to the bargaining process that takes place among the various parties whose (shaky) coalition is required for factors to be hired and for output to be produced and marketed. I stressed rather similarly the existence of obstacles to entrepreneurial and cooperative behavior needed for the making of development decisions.

Those who have found that the individual economic operators and, as a result, the economy are ordinarily far from doing as well as they might, can be expected to react to their shocking discovery along two principal lines. The immediate and most obvious reaction is a determined search for ways and means to take up the slack, to retrieve the ideal of the taut economy. As long as the pressures of competition do not seem to be sufficient, the pressures of adversity will be invoked.[13] Frequent changes in the environment, forcing the firm to be "on its toes," will be identified as one way of inducing performance closer to the firm's potential.[14] Insofar as innovation is concerned, the inducing and focusing virtues of strikes and war have been stressed.[15] My own search concentrated on pressure mechanisms such as intersectoral and intrasectoral imbalances and on production processes that exact high penalties for poor performance or do not tolerate it at all.[16] Finally, the advocates of social revolution have contributed to this line of thought: one of their most seductive arguments has long been that only revolutionary changes can tap and liberate the abundant but dormant, repressed, or alienated energies of the people.[17]

13. See Leibenstein, "Allocative Efficiency versus X-Efficiency."
14. Charles P. Bonini, "Simulation of Information and Decision Systems in the Firm" (unpub. diss. Carnegie Institute of Technology, 1962).
15. Nathan Rosenberg, "The Direction of Technological Change: Inducement Mechanisms and Focusing Devices," *Economic Development and Cultural Change*, 18 (October 1969).
16. Hirschman, *Strategy*, chs. 5–8.
17. See, for example, Paul Baran, *The Political Economy of Growth* (New York: Monthly Review Press, 1957).

Quite a different reaction to the discovery of slack occurs when the discoverer asks himself, after having got over his initial shock, whether slack may not after all be a good thing, a blessing in disguise. The idea that slack fulfills some important, if unintended or latent, functions was put forward by Cyert and March, who point out that it permits firms to ride out adverse market or other developments. During such bad times slack acts like a reserve that can be called upon: excess costs will be cut, innovations that were already within one's grasp will at last be introduced, more aggressive sales behavior that had been shunned will now be engaged in, and so on. Slack in the political system has been rationalized in a very similar manner. The discovery that citizens do not normally use more than a fraction of their political resources came originally as a surprise and disappointment to political scientists who had been brought up to believe that democracy requires for its functioning the fullest possible participation of all citizens. But soon enough a degree of apathy was found to have some compensating advantages in as much as it contributes to the stability and flexibility of a political system and provides for "reserves" of political resources which can be thrown into the battle in crisis situations.[18]

The immediate response to the discovery of slack has thus been either to assert the rationality of a certain level of slack or to look for ways of extirpating excessive levels by invoking exogenous forces such as adversity, imbalances, revolution, and so on. Both these approaches look at slack as a gap of a given magnitude between actual and potential performance of individuals, firms, and organizations. This book takes a further, more radical step in recognizing the importance and pervasiveness of slack. It assumes not only that slack has somehow come into the

18. See below, pp. 31–32.

world and exists in given amounts, but that it is *continuously being generated* as a result of some sort of entropy characteristic of human, surplus-producing societies. "There's a slacker born every minute," could be its motto. Firms and other organizations are conceived to be permanently and randomly subject to decline and decay, that is, to a gradual loss of rationality, efficiency, and surplus-producing energy, no matter how well the institutional framework within which they function is designed.

This radical pessimism, which views decay as an ever-present force constantly on the attack, generates its own cure: for as long as decay, while always conspicuous in some areas, is hardly in undisputed command everywhere and at all times, it is likely that the very process of decline activates certain counterforces.

## Exit and Voice as Impersonations of Economics and Politics

In examining the nature and strength of these endogenous forces of recovery, our inquiry bifurcates, as already explained. Its breakup into the two contrasting, though not mutually exclusive, categories of exit and voice would be suspiciously neat if it did not faithfully reflect a more fundamental schism: that between economics and politics. Exit belongs to the former realm, voice to the latter. The customer who, dissatisfied with the product of one firm, shifts to that of another, uses the market to defend his welfare or to improve his position; and he also sets in motion market forces which may induce recovery on the part of the firm that has declined in comparative performance. This is the sort of mechanism economics thrives on. It is neat—one either exits or one does not; it is impersonal —any face-to-face confrontation between customer and firm with its imponderable and unpredictable elements is avoided and success and failure of the organization are communicated to it by a set of statistics; and it is indirect —any recovery on the part of the declining firm comes by courtesy of the Invisible Hand, as an unintended by-product of the customer's decision to shift. In all these respects, voice is just the opposite of exit. It is a far more "messy" concept because it can be graduated, all the way from faint grumbling to violent protest; it implies articulation of one's critical opinions rather than a private, "secret" vote in the anonymity of a supermarket; and finally, it is direct and straightforward rather than roundabout. Voice is political action par excellence.

The economist tends naturally to think that his mechanism is far more efficient and is in fact the only one to be taken seriously. A particularly good illustration of this bias appears in a well-known essay by Milton Friedman which advocates the introduction of the market mechanism into public education. The essence of the Friedman proposal is the distribution of special-purpose vouchers to parents of school-age children; with these vouchers the parents could buy educational services that would be supplied in competition by private enterprise. In justifying this scheme he says:

Parents could express their views about schools *directly,* by withdrawing their children from one school and sending them to another, to a much greater extent than is now possible. In general they can now take this step only by changing their place of residence. *For the rest, they can express their views only through cumbrous political channels.*[19]

19. "The Role of Government in Education," in Robert A. Solo, ed., *Economics and the Public Interest* (New Brunswick, N.J.: Rutgers University Press, 1955), p. 129. A revised form of this essay was included in Friedman's *Capitalism and Freedom* (Chicago: University of Chicago Press, 1962) as ch. 6 and the cited passage appears unchanged on p. 91. The italics are mine.

I am not interested here in discussing the merits of the Friedman proposal.[20] Rather, I am citing the above passage as a near perfect example of the economist's bias in favor of exit and against voice. In the first place, Friedman considers withdrawal or exit as the "direct" way of expressing one's unfavorable views of an organization. A person less well trained in economics might naïvely suggest that the direct way of expressing views is to express them! Secondly, the decision to voice one's views and efforts to make them prevail are contemptuously referred to by Friedman as a resort to "cumbrous political channels." But what else is the political, and indeed the democratic, process than the digging, the use, and hopefully the slow improvement of these very channels?

In a whole gamut of human institutions, from the state to the family, voice, however "cumbrous," is all their members normally have to work with. Significantly, one major, if problem-plagued, effort presently underway toward better public schools in the large cities is to make them more responsive to their members: decentralization has been advocated and undertaken as a means of making the channels of communication between members and management in the public school systems less "cumbrous" than heretofore.

But the economist is by no means alone in having a blindspot, a "trained incapacity" (as Veblen called it) for perceiving the usefulness of one of our two mechanisms. In fact, in the political realm exit has fared much worse than has voice in the realm of economics. Rather than as merely ineffective or "cumbrous," exit has often been branded as *criminal,* for it has been labeled desertion, defection, and treason.

Clearly, passions and preconceptions must be reduced

20. For a good discussion see Henry M. Levin, "The Failure of the Public Schools and the Free Market Remedy," *The Urban Review,* 2:32–37 (June 1968).

on both sides if advantage is to be taken of an exceptional opportunity to observe how a typical market mechanism and a typical nonmarket, political mechanism work side by side, possibly in harmony and mutual support, possibly also in such a fashion that one gets into the other's way and undercuts its effectiveness.

A close look at this interplay between market and nonmarket forces will reveal the usefulness of certain tools of economic analysis for the understanding of political phenomena, *and vice versa*. Even more important, the analysis of this interplay will lead to a more complete understanding of social processes than can be afforded by economic or political analysis in isolation. From this point of view, this book can be viewed as the application to a new field of an argument on which much of *The Strategy of Economic Development* was based:

Tradition seems to require that economists argue forever about the question whether, in any disequilibrium situation, *market forces acting alone* are likely to restore equilibrium. Now this is certainly an interesting question. But as social scientists we surely must address ourselves also to the broader question: is the disequilibrium situation likely to be corrected at all, by market or nonmarket forces, or by both acting jointly? *It is our contention that nonmarket forces are not necessarily less "automatic" than market forces.*[21]

I was concerned here with disturbances of equilibrium and the return to it. Kenneth Arrow has argued along very similar lines for movements from less-than-optimal to optimal states:

I propose here the view that, when the market fails to achieve an optimal state, society will, to some extent at least, recognize the gap, and nonmarket social institutions

21. Hirschman, *Strategy*, p. 63. Italics in the original.

will arise attempting to bridge it . . . this process is not necessarily conscious.[22]

These views do not imply, as both Arrow and I immediately hastened to add, that any disequilibrium or nonoptimal state whatever will be eliminated by some combination of market and nonmarket forces. Nor do they exclude the possibility that the two sets of forces could work at cross-purposes. But they leave room for a conjunction—which could quite possibly be inadequate—of these two forces, whereas both laissez-faire and interventionist doctrines have looked at market and nonmarket forces in a strictly Manichaean way, it being understood that the laissez-faire advocate's forces of good are the interventionist's forces of evil and vice versa.

A final point. Exit and voice, that is, market and nonmarket forces, that is, economic and political mechanisms, have been introduced as two principal actors of strictly equal rank and importance. In developing my play on that basis I hope to demonstrate to political scientists the usefulness of economic concepts *and to economists the usefulness of political concepts.* This reciprocity has been lacking in recent interdisciplinary work as economists have claimed that concepts developed for the purpose of analyzing phenomena of scarcity and resource allocation can be successfully used for explaining political phenomena as diverse as power, democracy, and nationalism. They have thus succeeded in occupying large portions of the neighboring discipline while political scientists—whose inferiority complex vis-à-vis the tool-rich economist is equaled only by that of the economist vis-à-vis the physicist—have shown themselves quite eager to be colonized and have often actively joined the invaders. Perhaps it

22. "Uncertainty and the Welfare Economics of Medical Care," *American Economic Review,* 53:947 (December 1963).

takes an economist to reawaken feelings of identity and pride among our oppressed colleagues and to give them a sense of confidence that their concepts too have not only *grandeur,* but *rayonnement* as well? I like to think that this could be a by-product of the present essay.

# 2
# Exit

The availability to consumers of the exit option, and their frequent resort to it, are characteristic of "normal" (non-perfect) competition, where the firm has competitors but enjoys some latitude as both price-maker and quality-maker—and therefore, in the latter capacity, also as a quality-spoiler. As already mentioned, the exit option is widely held to be uniquely powerful: by inflicting revenue losses on delinquent management, exit is expected to induce that "wonderful concentration of the mind" akin to the one Samuel Johnson attributed to the prospect of being hanged.

Nevertheless the precise modus operandi of the exit option has not received much attention, to judge from a determined though inevitably fragmentary search of the vast literature on competition.[1] Most authors are content with general references to its "pressures" and "disciplines."

Insofar as the apologetic literature is concerned, this neglect of what could be considered one of the principal virtues of the "free enterprise system" may be particularly surprising; but some of the reasons for it have already been suggested. Those who celebrate the invigorating qualities of competition are loath to concede that the system could fail for even a single moment to make everybody perform at his peak form; should such a failure nevertheless occur in the case of some firm, that firm must *ipso facto* be assumed to be mortally sick and to be ready to leave the stage while some vigorous newcomer is presumably waiting in the wings to take its place. This "view of the American economy . . . as a biological process in which the old and the senile are continually being replaced by the young and the vigorous," as Galbraith puts it mock-

1. Which was carried out by David S. French.

ingly,[2] does not leave room for showing how competition helps to cure the temporary and remediable lapses whose importance is stressed here. It would seem that the apologists of competitive enterprise have missed, in their eagerness to stake extravagant claims for their system, one of the more substantial points to be made in its favor.

The technical economic literature, on the other hand, has been very largely concerned with discussing the conditions under which competitive market structures result or fail to result in an efficient allocation of resources within a static framework. One nonstatic aspect of competition has also been amply, if rather inconclusively, scrutinized, namely, its aptitude to generate innovation and growth. But, as far as I have been able to ascertain, no study, systematic or casual, theoretical or empirical, has been made of the related topic of competition's ability to lead firms back to "normal" efficiency, performance, and growth standards after they have lapsed from them.[3]

## How the Exit Option Works

The conceptual elements needed for such an exploration are straightforward. The first one is a variant of the

2. John Kenneth Galbraith, *American Capitalism: The Concept of Countervailing Power* (Boston: Houghton Mifflin Co., 1956), p. 36.

3. John Maurice Clark, who had a most lively sense of the multiplicity of functions competition is expected to perform, does mention that "another thing desired is that competition should keep firms vigilant to eliminate inefficiencies of process or product, before losses have so depleted their resources as to make rehabilitation difficult or impossible." *Competition as a Dynamic Process* (Washington: Brookings Institution, 1961), p. 81. In ch. 4, "What Do We Want Competition to Do for Us?" Clark dealt at some length with what he considered to be the ten principal functions of competition. Strangely, the rescue of faltering firms is not among them; the sentence cited is found, almost as an afterthought, at the end of a section entitled "Elimination of Inefficient Elements," which deals primarily with the "unpleasant services demanded of competition" in seeing to it that faltering firms are liquidated rather than restored to health.

familiar demand function, with the difference that quantity bought is made to depend on changes in quality rather than on price. Just as quality is normally assumed to remain unchanged when the effect of price changes on demand are considered, so it is now convenient to assume that price does not change when quality drops. Costs also remain constant, for by definition the quality decline results from a random lapse in efficiency rather than from a calculated attempt, on the part of the firm, to reduce costs by skimping on quality. Under these conditions, *any* exit whatever of consumers in response to quality decline will result in revenue losses; and, of course, the more massive the exit the greater the losses following upon any given quality drop. Whereas an increase in price can result in an increase in the firm's total revenue in spite of some customer exit, revenue can at best remain unchanged and will normally decline steadily as quality drops.[4]

Secondly, there exists a management reaction function which relates quality improvement to the loss in sales—upon finding out about customer desertion, management undertakes to repair its failings. Perhaps the simplest way to visualize such a relationship is as a discontinuous three-value function. No reaction occurs for a small drop in rev-

4. The response of demand and revenue to quality changes can be graphically represented by means of a demand curve with the familiar downward slope if the vertical axis of the traditional diagram is made to measure quality deterioration rather than price increase. This is done in Appendix A, figure 2, which also shows, in its lower portion, the effect of quality decline on revenue. This diagram makes clear that the effect on total revenue of a decline of demand caused by quality decline is much simpler—and more damaging—than that caused by price rises. In the former case, total revenue declines whenever the *quality*-elasticity of demand is greater than zero, whereas in the case of price increases total revenue falls of course only if *price*-elasticity of demand is greater than unity. (Unit elasticity of demand has no precise meaning in the case of quality-elasticity. When the concept of "quality-elasticity of demand" is put together in analogy to price-elasticity, two different scales—some measure of quality and money—are divided into one another. Hence, any numerical measure other than zero and infinity is the result of arbitrary scaling.)

enue, full recovery follows upon a drop of intermediate size; and, then again, if the revenue decline exceeds a certain large percentage of normal sales volume, no recuperation ensues—beyond a certain point, losses will weaken the firm so badly that bankruptcy will occur before any remedial measures can take effect.[5]

The interaction between the exit function and the reaction function can now be described. If there is to be a drop in quality it is desirable that it be of the size which leads to recuperation. Evidently if demand is highly inelastic with respect to quality change, revenue losses will be quite small and the firm will not get the message that something is amiss. But if demand is very elastic, the recuperation process will not take place either, this time because the firm will be wiped out before it will have had time to find out what hit it, much less to do something about it. This is a case of "too much, too soon." For the recuperation potential of the firm to come into play, it is therefore desirable that quality elasticity of demand be neither very large nor very small. This proposition, which is intuitively evident, can also be phrased as follows: For competition (exit) to work as a mechanism of recuperation from performance lapses, it is generally best for a firm to have a mixture of *alert* and *inert* customers. The alert customers provide the firm with a feedback mechanism which starts the effort at recuperation while the inert customers provide it with the time and dollar cushion needed for this effort to come to fruition. According to traditional notions,

5. It would be easy to think instead of a continuous reaction curve. Remedial action would be small with small sales losses and would then increase and later decline. It is even conceivable that, as a result of the reaction, the firm would come to produce at qualities superior to the ones at which it started out—to that extent one might speak of a point of "optimal deterioration" in quality. At a later point, beyond a certain loss in sales, the reaction would turn into reinforcement as demoralization and other results of financial stringency would compound quality deterioration and thus hasten the firm's downfall. Such a shape of the reaction function would not change materially the points that will be made in the text.

of course, the more alert the customers the better for the functioning of competitive markets. Consideration of competition as a recuperation mechanism reveals that, although exit of some customers is essential for bringing the mechanism into play, it is important that other customers remain unaware of, or unperturbed by, quality decline: if all were assiduous readers of *Consumer Reports*, or determined comparison shoppers, disastrous instability might result and firms would miss out on chances to recover from their occasional lapses.

As has already been noted, in perfect competition (which includes perfect consumer knowledge as one of its many exacting assumptions) the firm is not deprived of an effective correction mechanism because performance deterioration, which cannot possibly affect either quality or price, is reflected directly in a decline in revenue (due to increasing costs). But assume now a small departure from the perfectly competitive model so that the firm has some latitude in varying quality; then performance deterioration *can* (and is perhaps likely to) take the form of quality decline and if the market in which the firm sells is highly competitive, that is, full of highly knowledgeable buyers, the firm will be competed out of existence in very short order. In other words, while the perfectly competitive world is a feasible one from the point of view of an effective recuperation mechanism, the world of quasi-perfect competition is not. If one gives up, as he must in most real cases, the concept of a firm with no latitude as to quality whatever, then the optimal arrangement is not one as close as possible to that of perfect competition, but one rather far removed from it; and incremental moves in the direction of perfect competition are not necessarily improvements—the argument of the second best applies here in full force.

## Competition as Collusive Behavior

No matter what the quality elasticity of demand, exit could fail to cause any revenue loss to the individual firms *if the firm acquired new customers as it loses the old ones.* But why would a firm whose output deteriorates in quality attract any new customers at all? One can actually think of a situation in which this seemingly quite unlikely event would come to pass: when a uniform quality decline hits simultaneously all firms of an industry, each firm would garner in some of the disgruntled customers of the other firms while losing some of its previous customers to its competitors. In these circumstances the exit option is ineffective in alerting management to its failings, and a merger of all firms would appear to be socially desirable —that is, monopoly would replace competition to advantage, for customer dissatisfaction would then be vented directly and perhaps to some effect in attempts at improving the monopoly's management whereas under competition dissatisfaction takes the form of ineffective flitting back and forth of groups of consumers from one deteriorating firm to another without any firm getting a signal that something has gone awry.

While a simultaneous and uniform deterioration of all firms in a certain type of business is of course highly unlikely, a slight modification of the previous situation serves to endow it with greater realism and relevance. A competitively produced new product might reveal only through use some of its faults and noxious side-effects. In this case the claims of the various competing producers are likely to make for prolonged experimenting of consumers with alternate brands, all equally faulty, and hence for delay in bringing pressure on manufacturers for effective improvements in the product. Competition in this situation is a considerable convenience to the manufacturers because it keeps consumers from complaining; it diverts their energy to the hunting for the inexistent improved products that might possibly have been turned out by the competition. Under these circumstances, the manufacturers have a common interest in the maintenance rather than in the abridgement of competition—and may conceivably resort to collusive behavior to that end.[6]

The argument presented so far maintained the premise that the unsatisfactory features of the product turned out by the various competing firms could be eliminated as a result of pressures and a resultant search for solutions. But even if this premise is dropped, the competitive solution may again be inferior to one in which a single firm is the sole producer. For the presence of a number of competing firms fosters in this case the perpetual illusion that "the grass is always greener on the other side of the fence," that is, that an escape from defectiveness is possible through purchase of the competitor's product. Under monopoly, consumers would learn to live with inevitable imperfection and would seek happiness elsewhere than in the frantic search for the inexistent "improved" product.

The reader can judge whether elements of the foregoing situations can be detected in the economic and commercial life around us.[7] A few comments may be in order, however,

6. This is even more the case if the most determined comparison shoppers are those who would make most trouble for the manufacturers if there were no possibility of exit. The competitive mechanism then rids management of its potentially most troublesome customers. This argument is explained more fully below.

7. To help him judge I should like to provide some sample passages from letters recently fired off, by irate owners of "lemons," (a) to the Ford Motor Company: ". . . You can be assured that I absolutely will not purchase another Ford of any kind no matter what your usual form letter to me will say . . ." ". . . Needless to say my Falcon is the last of any Ford product I would consider to purchase. I am a young girl of 25, reasonably attractive, who has depleted her bank account buying Falcon transmissions, when there are other things in this world where the money could be put to much better use . . ."; and (b) to the General Motors Corporation: ". . . At home we have a Chevrolet bus and a Chevrolet van. You may be

on the relevance of the preceding notions for organizations other than business firms. The basic point is that competition may result merely in the mutual luring over of each others' customers on the part of a group of competing firms; and that to this extent competition and product diversification is wasteful and diversionary especially when, in its absence, consumers would either be able to bring more effective pressures upon management toward product improvement or would stop using up their energies in a futile search for the "ideal" product. It will be immediately evident that competitive political systems have frequently been portrayed in just these terms. Radical critics of societies with stable party systems have often denounced the competition of the dominant parties as offering "no real choice." It is of course a very open question whether, in the absence of the competitive party system, citizens would be better able to achieve fundamental social and political changes (assuming, for the sake of the argument, that such changes are desirable). Nevertheless the radical critique is correct in pointing out that competitive political systems have a considerable capacity to divert what might otherwise be a revolutionary ground swell into tame discontent with the governing party. Although this capacity may normally be an asset, one can surely conceive of circumstances under which it would turn into a liability.

A less speculative illustration of the issue under discussion can be drawn from the history of the trade union movement in this country. A preliminary step to the CIO-

---

sure that after all of this trouble and inconvenience and wasted time I shall never own a General Motors product again . . ." ". . . I have had a G.M. auto and wagon for many years now but maybe FORD has a better idea. I'll try to put up with this LEMON till the '70 models come out, but you can be sure there will be no G.M. product of any kind on my driveway . . ."

Copies of the letters from which these excerpts are taken were mailed by their authors to Ralph Nader who has kindly made them available to me.

AFL merger of 1955 was the No-Raiding Agreement which was concluded between the two organizations two years earlier. The text of this agreement referred to a statistical study of all petitions over a two-year period, addressed by CIO-AFL unions to the National Labor Relations Board for certification as the official bargaining agents in industrial plants. It was found that most petitions were unsuccessful and that those which were granted were about equally divided between CIO petitions to displace an AFL union and AFL petitions to displace a CIO union. These results, so the report says, "compel the conclusion that raids between AFL and CIO unions are destructive of the best interests of the unions immediately involved and also of the entire trade union movement." [8] As reasons for this conclusion, the document cites unrest and disunity created among the workers as a result of the raids, successful or not, and the desirability of devoting the energies of the trade union movement to the organization of unaffiliated workers rather than to raiding. Implicit in this conclusion is the judgment that the disadvantages of exit-competition outweighed in this case its possible efficiency-inducing advantages and *perhaps* the assumption that these advantages can be better secured via the alternative mechanism—voice—which must now be examined more closely.

8. American Federation of Labor and Congress of Industrial Organizations, *Constitution of the AFL-CIO* (Washington, D.C., January 1956), AFL-CIO Publication no. 2, p. 36. I am indebted to John Dunlop for the reference and for discussing this point with me.

29

# 3
# Voice

If the exit option has not been investigated in detail by economists, its existence and effect on performance—generally presumed to be wholesome—nevertheless underlies many judgments and attitudes toward economic institutions. Nothing remotely similar can be said about the voice option. The very idea that this is another "recuperation mechanism" which can come into play alongside, or in lieu of, the exit option is likely to be met with a mixture of incredulity and raised eyebrows. Yet, in this age of protest, it has become quite apparent that dissatisfied consumers (or members of an organization), rather than just go over to the competition, can "kick up a fuss" and thereby force improved quality or service upon delinquent management. It is therefore both legitimate and timely to examine the conditions under which the voice option is likely to make an effective appearance, either as a complement to exit or as a substitute for it.

To resort to voice, rather than exit, is for the customer or member to make an attempt at changing the practices, policies, and outputs of the firm from which one buys or of the organization to which one belongs. Voice is here defined as any attempt at all to change, rather than to escape from, an objectionable state of affairs, whether through individual or collective petition to the management directly in charge, through appeal to a higher authority with the intention of forcing a change in management, or through various types of actions and protests, including those that are meant to mobilize public opinion.

It is becoming clear, as was already pointed out in the introductory chapter, that voice is nothing but a basic portion and function of any political system, known sometimes also as "interest articulation." [1] Political scientists

1. For a recent treatment in a comparative perspective see G. A. Almond and G. B. Powell, Jr., *Comparative Politics: A Developmental Approach* (Boston: Little, Brown and Co., 1966), ch. 4.

have long dealt systematically with this function and its various manifestations. But in doing so they have ordinarily confined their attention to situations in which the only alternative to articulation is aquiescence or indifference (rather than exit), while economists have refused to consider that the discontented consumer might be anything but either dumbly faithful or outright traitorous (to the firm he used to do business with). A niche thus exists for this book, which affirms that the choice is often between articulation and "desertion"—voice and exit, in our neutral terminology.

First a few remarks on the working of voice in isolation, as compared to that of exit. As before, the initial assumption is a decline in the performance of a firm or organization which is remediable provided the attention of management is sufficiently focused on the task. If conditions are such that the decline leads to voice rather than to exit on the part of the discontented member-customers, then the effectiveness of voice will increase, up to a certain point, with its volume. But voice is like exit in that it can be overdone: the discontented customers or members could become so harassing that their protests would at some point hinder rather than help whatever efforts at recovery are undertaken. For reasons that will become clear this is most unlikely to happen in relations between customers and business firms; but in the realm of politics—the more characteristic province of voice—the possibility of negative returns to voice making their appearance at some point is by no means to be excluded.

An interesting parallel appears here between economics and exit, on the one hand, and politics and voice, on the other. Just as in economics it had long been thought that the more elastic demand is (that is, the more rapidly exit ensues whenever deterioration occurs) the better for the functioning of the economic system, so it has long been an article of faith of political theory that the proper functioning of democracy requires a maximally alert, active, and vocal public. In the United States, this belief was shaken by empirical studies of voting and political behavior which demonstrated the existence of considerable political apathy on the part of large sections of the public, for long periods of time.[2] Since the democratic system appeared to survive this apathy rather well, it became clear that the relations between political activism of the citizens and stable democracy are considerably more complex than had once been thought. As in the case of exit, a mixture of alert and inert citizens, or even an alternation of involvement and withdrawal, may actually serve democracy better than either total, permanent activism or total apathy. One reason, stressed by Robert Dahl, is that the ordinary failure, on the part of most citizens, to use their potential political resources to the full makes it possible for them to react with unexpected vigor—by using normally unused reserves of political power and influence—whenever their vital interests are directly threatened.[3] According to another line of reasoning, the democratic political system requires "blending of apparent contradictions": on the one hand, the citizen must express his point of view so that the political elites know and can be responsive to what he wants, but, on the other, these elites must be allowed to make decisions. The citizen must thus be in turn influential and deferential.[4]

2. See Robert A. Dahl, *Modern Political Analysis* (Englewood Cliffs, N.J.: Prentice-Hall, Inc., 1966), ch. 6 for data and principal sources.

3. Robert A. Dahl, *Who Governs?* (New Haven: Yale University Press, 1961), pp. 309–310. This point is remarkably similar to the one made by March and Cyert about the virtues of "organizational slack" in the economic system. See *The Behavioral Theory of the Firm* (Englewood Cliffs, N.J.: Prentice-Hall, Inc., 1963), pp. 36–38.

4. Gabriel A. Almond and Sidney Verba, *The Civic Culture: Political Attitudes and Democracy in Five Nations* (Boston: Little, Brown and Co., 1965), pp. 338–344. A similar thought is expressed by Robert Lane who shows that, in certain respects, "one can assign different political roles to the political activists and the indifferents and that a balance between the two can achieve beneficient results." *Political Life* (New York: Free Press of Glencoe, Inc., 1959), p. 345.

The essential reasoning behind this thesis is quite similar to the argument made earlier on the need for exit to stay within certain bounds. Voice has the function of alerting a firm or organization to its failings, but it must then give management, old or new, some time to respond to the pressures that have been brought to bear on it.

Finally, then, the relation between voice and improvement in an organization's efficiency has considerable similarity with the modus operandi of exit. This does not mean, however, that exit and voice will always both have positive effects at first and destructive ones at a later stage. In the case of any one particular firm or organization and its deterioration, either exit or voice will ordinarily have the role of the *dominant* reaction mode. The subsidiary mode is then likely to show up in such limited volume that it will never become destructive for the simple reason that, if deterioration proceeds, the job of destruction is accomplished single-handedly by the dominant mode. In the case of normally competitive business firms, for example, exit is clearly the dominant reaction to deterioration and voice is a badly underdeveloped mechanism; it is difficult to conceive of a situation in which there would be too much of it.

## Voice as a Residual of Exit

The voice option is the only way in which dissatisfied customers or members can react whenever the exit option is unavailable. This is very nearly the situation in such basic social organizations as the family, the state, or the church. In the economic sphere, the theoretical construct of pure monopoly would spell a no-exit situation, but the mixture of monopolistic and competitive elements characteristic of most real market situations should make it possible to observe the voice option in its interaction with the exit option.

33

We return to the simple relationship between deterioration of a product and declining sales, but look now at those who continue as customers. While they are not yet ready to desert the firm, they are likely to experience different degrees of unhappiness about the quality decline. Being presumably endowed with some capacity to articulate this discontent, these nonexiting customers are therefore the source of the voice option. The other determinant of voice is of course the degree of discontent of the nonexiting customer which depends roughly on the degree of deterioration.

In a first approximation, then, voice can be viewed as a residual. Whoever does not exit is a candidate for voice and voice depends, like exit, on the quality elasticity of demand. But the direction of the relationship is turned around: with a given potential for articulation, the actual level of voice feeds on *in*elastic demand, or on the lack of opportunity for exit.[5]

In this view, the role of voice would increase as the opportunities for exit decline, up to the point where, with exit wholly unavailable, voice must carry the entire burden of alerting management to its failings. That such a see-saw relationship between exit and voice exists in fact to some extent is illustrated by the many complaints about quality and service that have been prominently published for years in the Soviet press. With exit-competition playing a much smaller role in the Soviet economy than in the market economies of the West, it was found necessary to give voice a more prominent role.

Similarly, voice is in a much more commanding position in less developed countries where one simply cannot choose between as many commodities, nor between as many varieties of the same good, nor between as many ways of traveling from one point of the country to another, as in an

5. The relationship between the volumes of exit and voice that is indicated here is spelled out in more formal terms in Appendix A.

advanced economy. Therefore, the atmosphere in the former countries is more suffused with loud, often politically colored protests against poor quality of goods or services than it is in the advanced countries where dissatisfaction is more likely to take the form of silent exit.

Turning now to the reaction function, that is, to the effect of voice on recuperation of efficiency on the part of voice-exposed management, we shall assume that exit is the dominant reaction mode. In a preliminary appraisal of the combined effect of exit and voice, the possibility of voice having a destructive rather than constructive effect may therefore be excluded. Obviously sales losses and complaints or protests of those who remain members are not easily added to derive an aggregate recuperative effect.[6] Both the propensity to protest and the effectiveness of complaints vary widely from one firm-customer complex to another. But three general statements can be made:

(1) In the simple model presented up to now, voice functions as a complement to exit, not as a substitute for it. Whatever voice is forthcoming under those conditions is a net gain from the point of view of the recuperation mechanism.[7]

6. Voice may cause direct monetary losses to the firm, as, for example, when dissatisfied consumers are able to turn in defective merchandise. If voice appears exclusively in this particular incarnation, then its likely effectiveness in making an impression on profit-conscious managers can be precisely measured against that of exit. See Appendix A.

7. Voice could usefully complement competition also in a more familiar context. Economists who have hopefully eyed competition's ability to allocate resources efficiently have generally concluded that the most serious impediment to the hope's fulfillment is the existence of external diseconomies in production and consumption (pollution, littering of beaches with beer cans, and so forth). Obviously, these diseconomies could be contained or prevented through effective articulation of protests on the part of those who suffer from them. In other words, the voice of the nonconsumer on whom the diseconomies are inflicted could become a valuable adjunct to the competitive mechanism. Once this is realized it is perhaps less surprising that the voice of the *consumer* too has a role to play in complementing the mechanism.

(2) The more effective voice is (the effectiveness of exit being given), the more quality-inelastic can demand be without the chances for recuperation stemming from exit and voice *combined* being impaired.

(3) Considering that beyond a certain point, exit has a destructive rather than salutary effect, the optimal pattern from the point of view of maximizing the combined effectiveness of exit and voice over the whole process of deterioration may be an elastic response of demand to the first stages of deterioration and an inelastic one for the later stages. This pattern has long been held to be characteristic of consumer responses to price increases for certain commodities which are vitally needed in limited quantities even at high prices, but whose consumption will easily expand beyond this point if prices drop. It may similarly apply to quality elasticity of demand, especially if the only alternative available for a deteriorating product is a higher-priced substitute. Eventually, of course, as quality becomes abominable, demand will vanish (just as it does, because of the budget constraint, when price increases indefinitely), but there may well be a number of goods and services whose demand will move from quality-elastic to quality-inelastic for a wide range of quality declines. The reason for which even such a pattern may be too much weighted by exit will be commented on at some length in Chapter 4.

## Voice as an Alternative to Exit [8]

Up to now, the treatment of voice has suffered from a certain timidity: the new concept has been viewed as wholly subordinated to exit. In judging the volume of voice to be determined by the quality elasticity of demand, one implicitly assumes that customers who are faced by

8. See Appendix B for a more technical discussion of the topics treated in this section.

a decline in quality first decide whether to shift to another firm or product regardless of their ability to influence the behavior of the firm from which they usually buy; only if they do not shift, does it possibly occur to them to make a fuss. If the matter is put in this way it is immediately evident, however, that the decision whether to exit will often be taken *in the light of the prospects for the effective use of voice*. If customers are sufficiently convinced that voice will be effective, then they may well *postpone* exit. Hence, quality-elasticity of demand, and therefore exit, can also be viewed as depending on the ability and willingness of the customers to take up the voice option. It may, in fact, be more appropriate to put matters in this way, for if deterioration is a process unfolding in stages over a period of time, the voice option is more likely to be taken at an early stage. Once you have exited, you have lost the opportunity to use voice, but not vice versa; in some situations, exit will therefore be a reaction of *last resort* after voice has failed.

It appears, therefore, that voice can be a substitute for exit, as well as a complement to it. What are the conditions, then, under which voice will be preferred to exit? The question can be formulated more precisely as follows: If a competing or substitute product $B$ is available at the same price as the normally bought product $A$ and if, because of the deterioration of $A$, $B$ is now clearly superior from the point of view of $A$'s customers, under what conditions will a customer of $A$ *fail* to go over to $B$?

Once voice is viewed as a substitute for exit, an important component of the voice option consists in this decision to continue as a customer of the deteriorating and now inferior product (or as a member of the deteriorating organization), for it will presumably be taken only by those who wish for and expect $A$ to recover its original superiority over $B$, and not necessarily by all of them. Ordinarily, a customer or member will undergo the sacrifice of staying with $A$ because he feels that he wants and is able to "do something" about $A$ and because only by remaining a customer or member will he be able to exert this influence. Nevertheless, the decision not to exit in the face of a clearly better buy (or organization) could also be taken by customers (or members) who expect the complaints and protests of *others*, combined with their own faithfulness, to be successful. Others may not care to switch to $B$ when they feel that they would soon want to switch back, because of the costs that may be involved. Finally there are those who stay with $A$ out of "loyalty," that is, in a less rational, though far from wholly irrational, fashion.[9] Many of these "loyalists" will actively participate in actions designed to change $A$'s policies and practices, but some may simply refuse to exit and suffer in silence, confident that things will soon get better. Thus the voice option includes vastly different degrees of activity and leadership in the attempt to achieve change "from within." But it always involves the decision to "stick" with the deteriorating firm or organization and this decision is in turn based on:

(1) an evaluation of the chances of getting the firm or organization producing $A$ "back on the track," through one's own action or through that of others; and

(2) a judgment that it is worthwhile, for a variety of reasons, to trade the certainty of $B$ which is available here and now against these chances.

This view of the matter shows the substitutability of $B$ for $A$ as an important element in the decision to resort to voice, but as only one of several elements. Naturally, the consumer will resort to voice if $A$'s original margin of superiority over $B$ was wide enough to make it worthwhile for him to forego a $B$ that is superior right here and now. That will hardly ever be the case if $A$ and $B$ are very close substitutes. But given a minimum of nonsubstituta-

9. See ch. 7, below.

bility, voice will depend also on the willingness to take the chances of the voice option as against the certainty of the exit option and on the probability with which a consumer expects improvements to occur as a result of actions to be taken by himself or by others with him or just by others.

It is useful to compare this formulation with the related one provided by Edward Banfield in his study of political influence: "The effort an interested party makes to put its case before the decisionmaker will be in proportion *to the advantage to be gained from a favorable outcome multiplied by the probability of influencing the decision.*[10]

Banfield derived this rule from his study of public policy decisions in a large American city and of the participation of various groups and individuals in the decisionmaking process. He, like most political scientists looking at the "articulation-of-interests" function, was analyzing situations in which individuals or groups had essentially the choice between passivity and involvement. The present model is more complicated because it allows for exit, as a result of the availability of a substitute product. Banfield's formulation correctly states the benefits of the voice option,[11] but for our purposes there is need to introduce cost which so far has been identified as the foregoing of the exit option. In fact, in addition to this opportunity cost, account must be taken of the direct cost of voice which is incurred as buyers of a product or members of an organization spend time and money in the attempt to achieve changes in the policies and practices of the firm from which they buy or of the organization to which they belong. Not nearly so high a cost is likely to be attached to the exercise of the exit option in the case of products

10. Edward C. Banfield, *Political Influence* (New York: Free Press of Glencoe, 1961), p. 333. Italics in the original.
11. It should be noted that our concept of voice, as defined at the beginning of this chapter, is much wider than Banfield's "influence," which appears to exclude any expression of opinion or discontent that is not addressed directly to the officeholding decisionmaker.

bought in the market—although some allowance should be made for the possible loss of loyalty discounts and for the cost of obtaining information about substitute products to which one intends to switch.[12]

Hence, in comparison to the exit option, voice is costly and conditioned on the influence and bargaining power customers and members can bring to bear within the firm from which they buy or the organizations to which they belong. These two characteristics point to roughly similar areas of economic and social life in which voice is likely to play an important role and to hold exit at bay, at least for a time. As voice tends to be costly in comparison to exit, the consumer will become less able to afford voice as the number of goods and services over which he spreads his purchases increases—the cost of devoting even a modicum of his time to correcting the faults of any one of the entities he is involved with is likely to exceed his estimate of the expected benefits for a large number of them. This is also one of the reasons for which voice plays a more important role with respect to *organizations* of which an individual is a member than with respect to *firms* whose products he buys: the former are far less numerous than the latter. In addition, of course, the proliferation of products tends to increase cross-elasticities of demand and to that extent it would increase the probability of exit for a given deterioration in quality of any one product picked at random. For these reasons, voice is likely to be an active mechanism primarily with respect to the more substantial purchases and organizations in which buyers and members are involved.

Similar conclusions with respect to the *locus* of the voice option are reached when one focuses on the other characteristic which distinguishes voice from exit, namely, the requirement that a customer must expect that he himself

12. When loyalty is present, however, the cost of exit may be substantial. The point will be discussed in ch. 7, below.

or other member-customers will be able to marshal some influence or bargaining power. Obviously, this is not the case in atomistic markets. Voice is most likely to function as an important mechanism in markets with few buyers or where a few buyers account for an important proportion of total sales, both because it is easier for few buyers than for many to combine for collective action and simply because each one may have much at stake and wield considerable power even in isolation.[13] Again, it is more common to encounter influential members of an organization than buyers with a great deal of influence on the policies of firms from which they buy,[14] and the voice option will therefore be observed more frequently among organizations than among business firms.

Certain types of purchases may nevertheless lend themselves particularly to the voice option, even though many buyers are involved. When the consumer has been dissatisfied with an inexpensive, nondurable good, he will most probably go over to a different variety without making a fuss. But if he is stuck with an expensive durable good such as an automobile which disappoints him day-in and day-out, he is much less likely to remain silent. And his complaints will be of some concern to the firm or dealer whose product he has bought both because he remains a potential customer in one, three, or five years' time and because adverse word-of-mouth propaganda is powerful in the case of standardized goods.

The upshot of this discussion for the comparative roles of voice and exit at various stages of economic development is two-edged: the sheer number of available goods and varieties in an advanced economy favors exit over voice, but the increasing importance in such an economy

13. See Mancur Olson, Jr., *The Logic of Collective Action* (Cambridge, Mass.: Harvard University Press, 1965).

14. See, however, the description of the influential buyer in John Kenneth Galbraith, *American Capitalism: The Concept of Countervailing Power* (Boston: Houghton Mifflin Co., 1956), pp. 117–123.

of standardized durable consumer goods requiring large outlays works in the opposite direction.

Although the foregoing remarks restrict the domain in which the voice option is likely to be deployed, especially as a substitute for exit, the territory left to it remains both considerable and somewhat ill-defined. Moreover, once voice is recognized as a mechanism with considerable usefulness for maintaining performance, institutions can be designed in such a way that the cost of individual and collective action would be decreased. Or, in some situations, the rewards for *successful* action might be increased for those who had initiated it.

Often it is possible to create entirely new channels of communication for groups, such as consumers, which have had notorious difficulties in making their voice heard, in comparison to other interest groups. Consumers have, in fact, made such progress in this regard that there is now talk of a "consumer revolution" as part of the general "participation explosion." The former phrase does not refer to the long established and still quite useful consumer research organizations, but to the more militant actions by or on behalf of consumers that have been taken recently, the most spectacular and resourceful being the campaigns of Ralph Nader, who has established himself as a sort of self-appointed consumer ombudsman.[15] The appointment since 1964 of a consumer adviser to the President has been a response to this emergence of the consumer voice which was quite unexpected in an economy where competition-exit is supposed to solve most of the "sovereign" consumer's problems. As a result of these developments, it looks as though consumer voice will be institutionalized at three levels: through independent entrepreneurship à la Nader, through revitalization of

15. The broad range of Nader's work, with respect to both products and action, is brought out in his article "The Great American Gyp," *The New York Review of Books*, November 21, 1968.

official regulatory agencies, and through stepped-up preventive activities on the part of the more important firms selling to the public.[16]

The creation of effective new channels through which consumers can communicate their dissatisfaction holds one important lesson. While structural constraints (availability of close substitutes, number of buyers, durability and standardization of the article, and so forth) are of undoubted importance in determining the balance of exit and voice for individual commodities, the propensity to resort to the voice option depends also on the general readiness of a population to complain and on the *invention* of such institutions and mechanisms as can communicate complaints cheaply and effectively. Recent experience even raises some doubts whether the structural constraints deserve to be called "basic" when they can suddenly be overcome by a single individual such as Ralph Nader.[17]

Thus, while exit requires nothing but a clearcut either-or decision, voice is essentially an *art* constantly evolving in new directions. This situation makes for an important bias in favor of exit when both options are present: customer-members will ordinarily base their decision on *past* experience with the cost and effectiveness of voice even though the possible *discovery* of lower cost and greater effectiveness is of the very essence of voice. The presence of the exit alternative can therefore tend to *atrophy the development of the art of voice*. This is a central point of this book which will be argued from a different angle in the next chapter.

16. Traditionally such firms have been engaged in considerable "auscultation" of voice through market surveys.

17. For another, most vivid case in point, within the context of community action in Venezuela, see Lisa Redfield Peattie, *The View from the Barrio* (Ann Arbor, Mich.: University of Michigan Press, 1968), ch. 7; the "art" of eliciting voice, this time in low-income neighborhoods of American cities, is also the subject of her article "Reflections on Advocacy Planning," *Journal of the American Institute of Planners* (March 1968), pp. 80–88.

# 4
# A Special Difficulty
# in Combining
# Exit and Voice

The groundwork has now been laid for telling the reader about the empirical observation that was mentioned in the Preface as the origin of this essay. In a recent book, I tried to explain why the Nigerian railways had performed so poorly in the face of competition from trucks, even for such long-haul, bulky cargo as peanuts (which are grown in Northern Nigeria, some eight hundred miles from the ports of Lagos and Port d'Harcourt). Specific economic, socio-political, and organizational reasons could be found for the exceptional ability of the trucks to get the better of the railroads in the Nigerian environment; but having done so I still had to account for the prolonged incapacity of the railroad administration to correct some of its more glaring inefficiencies, *in spite of active competition,* and proposed the following explanation:

The presence of a ready alternative to rail transport makes it less, rather than more, likely that the weaknesses of the railways will be fought rather than indulged. With truck and bus transportation available, a deterioration in rail service is not nearly so serious a matter as if the railways held a monopoly for long-distance transport—it can be lived with for a long time without arousing strong public pressures for the basic and politically difficult or even explosive reforms in administration and management that would be required. This may be the reason public enterprise, not only in Nigeria but in many other countries, has strangely been at its weakest in sectors such as transportation and education where it is subjected to competition: instead of stimulating improved or top performance, the presence of a ready and satisfactory substitute for the services public enterprise offers merely deprives it of a precious feedback mechanism that operates at its best when the customers are securely locked in. For the management of public enterprise, always fairly confident that it will not be let down by the national treasury, may be less sensitive to the loss of revenue due to the switch of customers to a competing mode than to the protests of an aroused public that has a vital stake in the service, has no alternative, and will therefore "raise hell." [1]

In Nigeria, then, I had encountered a situation where the combination of exit and voice was particularly noxious for any recovery: exit did not have its usual attention-focusing effect because the loss of revenue was not a matter of the utmost gravity for management, while voice did not work as long as the most aroused and therefore the potentially most vocal customers were the first ones to abandon the railroads for the trucks. It is particularly this last phenomenon that must be looked at more closely, for if it has any generality, then the chances that voice will ever act in conjunction with exit would be poor and voice would be an effective recuperation mechanism only in conditions of full monopoly "when the customers are securely locked in."

As a preliminary to generalizing about this sort of situation, another example, closer to home, may be helpful. If public and private schools somewhere in the United States are substituted in the story for the railroads and lorries of Nigeria, a rather similar result follows. Suppose at some point, for whatever reason, the public schools deteriorate. Thereupon, increasing numbers of quality-education-conscious parents will send their children to private schools.[2] This "exit" may occasion some impulse toward an improvement of the public schools; but here again this im-

1. *Development Projects Observed* (Washington: Brookings Institution, 1967), pp. 146–147.

2. Private schools being costly and income distribution unequal, the public schools will of course be deserted primarily by the wealthier parents. Nevertheless, the willingness to make a financial sacrifice for the sake of improving the children's education differs widely within a given income class, especially at intermediate levels of income. In its pure form, the phenomenon here described is best visualized for a school district with many middle-class parents for whom

pulse is far less significant than the loss to the public schools of those member-customers who would be most motivated and determined to put up a fight against the deterioration if they did not have the alternative of the private schools.

In the preceding examples, insensitivity to exit is exhibited by public agencies that can draw on a variety of financial resources outside and independent of sales revenue. But situations in which exit is the predominant reaction to decline while voice might be more efficacious in arresting it can also be observed in the sphere of private business enterprise. The relation between corporate management and the stockholders is a case in point. When the management of a corporation deteriorates, the first reaction of the best-informed stockholders is to look around for the stock of better-managed companies. In thus orienting themselves toward exit, rather than toward voice, investors are said to follow the Wall Street rule that "if you do not like the management you should sell your stock." According to a well-known manual this rule "results in perpetuating bad management and bad policies." Naturally it is not so much the Wall Street rule that is at fault as the ready availability of alternative investment opportunities in the stock market which makes any resort to voice rather than to exit unthinkable for any but the most committed stockholder.[3]

---

the decision to send the children to private school is a significant, yet tolerable burden.

3. The passages in quotes are from B. Graham and D. L. Dodd, *Security Analysis*, 3d ed. (New York: McGraw-Hill, 1951), p. 616. The argument is spelled out in some detail in ch. 50, "Stockholder-Management Controversies." In the fourth edition of this work (1962), the authors return only briefly to this argument, and seem to be aware that the institutional odds are heavily stacked against any substantial success of their exhortations: "In quixotic fashion perhaps," they say wistfully, "we wanted to combat the traditional but harmful notion that if a stockholder doesn't like the way his company is run he should sell his shares, no matter how low their price may be" (p. 674).

While it is most clearly revealed in the private-public school case, one characteristic is crucial in all of the foregoing situations: those customers who care *most* about the quality of the product and who, therefore, are those who would be the most active, reliable, and creative agents of voice are for that very reason also those who are apparently likely to exit first in case of deterioration.

One interest of this observation is that it could define a whole class of economic structures where a tight monopoly would be preferable, within the framework of the "slack" or "fallible" economy, to competition. But before jumping to this conclusion, we must take a closer look at the observation by translating it into the ordinary language of economic analysis.

In terms of that language, the situations just described have more than a faint odor of paradox. We all know that when the price of a commodity goes up, it is the *marginal* customer, the one with the smallest consumer surplus, the one, that is, who cares *least,* who drops out first. How is it then that with a decline in quality the opposite seems quite plausible: *Is it possible that the consumers who drop out first as price increases are not the same as those who exit first when quality declines?* [4] If this question were to be answered in the affirmative, it would be easier to understand why combining exit and voice is so troublesome in some situations.

The basic reason for our paradox lies in the still insufficiently explored role of quality (as contrasted with price) in economic life. Traditional demand analysis is overwhelmingly in terms of price and quantity, categories which have the immense advantage of being recorded, measurable, and finely divisible. Quality changes have usually been dealt with by economists and statisticians

4. Appendix C refers to this possibility as the "reversal phenomenon." The discussion in the following pages should be read in conjunction with Appendixes C and D by those who find diagrams clearer than language.

through the concept of the *equivalent* price or quantity change. An article of poor quality can often be considered to be simply less in quantity than the same article of standard quality; this is the case, for example, of the automobile tire which lasts on the average only half as long (in terms of mileage) as a high quality tire. Alternatively, poor quality can often be translated into higher costs and prices; for example, increased pilferage in the rendering of railroad freight service will result in higher insurance premiums. In the latter case, a large part of the quality deterioration can be described by the statement: "now everybody really pays more for the same railroad service than before." To the extent that this statement is correct, there would be no reason to expect the effect of quality deterioration on demand (that is, for who gets out first) to be any different from the effect of a uniform rise in price. In other words, if a quality decline can be fully expressed as an equivalent rise in price that is *uniform for all buyers* of the article, the effects on customer exit of the quality decline and of the equivalent rise in price would be identical.

The crucial point can now be made. For any one individual, a quality change can be translated into equivalent price change. But this equivalence *is frequently different for different customers of the article because appreciation of quality differs widely among them.* This is so to some extent even in the just mentioned case of automobile tires and of increased pilferage of freight sent by rail. Appreciation of the longer life of quality tires will depend on the time discount of each individual buyer. In the case of rail freight, the increase in the insurance premium fully offsets only the increase in average direct monetary costs which is occasioned to the shipper by the worsening in service. For some shippers this may be all they care about, but there will surely be others for whom the lessened reliability of rail service represents costs (in inconvenience, reputation of their own reliability, and so forth) that cannot be fully made good through an insurance scheme. That appreciation of quality—of wine, cheese, or of education for one's children—differs widely among different groups of people is surely no great discovery. It implies, however, that a given deterioration in quality will inflict very different losses (that is, different equivalent price increases) on different customers; someone who had a very high consumer surplus before deterioration precisely because he is a connoisseur and would be willing to pay, say, twice the actual price of the article at its original quality, may drop out as a customer as soon as quality deteriorates, provided a nondeteriorated competing product is available, be it at a much higher price.

Here, then, is the rationale for our observation: in the case of "connoisseur goods"—and, as the example of education indicates, this category is by no means limited to quality wines—the consumers who drop out when quality declines are not necessarily the marginal consumers who would drop out if price increased, but may be intramarginal consumers with considerable consumer surplus; or, put more simply, the consumer who is rather insensitive to price increases is often likely to be highly sensitive to quality declines.

At the same time, consumers with a high consumer surplus are, for that very reason, those who have most to lose through a deterioration of the product's quality. Therefore, they are the ones who are most likely to make a fuss in case of deterioration until such time as they do exit. "You can actively flee, then, and you can actively stay put." This phrase of Erik Erikson [5] applies with full force to the choice that is typically made by the quality-conscious consumer or the member who cares deeply about the policies pursued by the organization to which he be-

5. *Insight and Responsibility* (New York: W. W. Norton & Co., Inc., 1964), p. 86.

longs. To make that kind of consumer and member "actively stay put" for a while should be a matter of considerable concern for many firms and organizations, and particularly for those, of course, that respond more readily to voice than to exit.

Before the varieties of consumer behavior in the case of connoisseur goods are further explored, a brief homage to the hoary concept of consumer surplus is in order, for it appears to have the useful property of measuring the potential for the exercise of influence on the part of different consumers. This potential is the counterpart of the concept's traditional content. Consumer surplus measures the gain to the consumer of being able to buy a product at its market price: the larger that gain the more likely is it that the consumer will be motivated to "do something" to have that gain safeguarded or restored. In this way it is possible to derive the chances for political action from a concept that has dwelt so far exclusively in the realm of economic theory.[6]

Evidently the nature of the available substitute has something to do with the question whether or not connoisseur goods will be rapidly forsaken, in case of deterioration, by the more quality-conscious customers. In the discussion of the exit and voice options in Chapter 3, it was assumed that the only available competing or substitute good was initially of inferior quality, but carried the same price tag. Usually, of course, many other combinations of price and quality exist: in particular, consumers may often have had some hesitation between the good they actually bought, a better-quality substitute with a higher price, and a poorer-quality substitute with a lower price. Suppose now that only the former type of substitute exists

6. For a similar transformation of a time-honored economic concept, the gain from trade, into a political category, namely the influence a trading partner may acquire in the gain-receiving country, see my *National Power and the Structure of Foreign Trade* (Berkeley: University of California Press, 1945, rev. ed. 1969), ch. 2.

and that the quality of the connoisseur good normally bought by a group of consumers deteriorates. In this case it is immediately plausible that the consumers who valued the deteriorating good most will be the first ones to decide that it is worth their while to go over to the higher-quality, higher-price substitute. If only a lower-price, lower-quality good is available, on the other hand, these highly quality-conscious consumers, even though they suffer greatly as a result of quality deterioration, will stick with it longer than their less quality-conscious colleagues. These and similar propositions can be easily proved by indifference curve analysis.[7]

Hence the rapid exit of the highly quality-conscious customers—a situation which paralyzes voice by depriving it of its principal agents—is tied to the availability of better-quality substitutes at higher prices. Such a situation has, for example, been observed in the field of housing. When general conditions in a neighborhood deteriorate, those who value most highly neighborhood qualities such as safety, cleanliness, good schools, and so forth will be the first to move out; they will search for housing in somewhat more expensive neighborhoods or in the suburbs and will be lost to the citizens' groups and community action programs that would attempt to stem and reverse the tide of deterioration. Reverting to the public-private school case, it now appears that the "lower-priced" public schools have several strikes against them in their competition with private schools: first, if and when there is a deterioration in the quality of public school education these schools will lose the children of those highly quality-conscious parents who might otherwise have fought deterioration; second, if, thereafter, quality comes to decline in the private schools, then this type of parents will keep their children there for much longer than was the case

7. See Appendix D, which also discusses in more technical terms a number of other points made in this section.

when the public schools deteriorated. Hence, when public and private schools coexist, with the quality of education in the latter being higher, deterioration will be more strenuously fought "from within" in the case of the private than in that of the public schools. And because exit is not a particularly powerful recuperation mechanism in the case of public schools—it is far more so in that of private schools which have to make ends meet—the failure of one of our two mechanisms is here compounded by the inefficiency of the other.

The relevance of the foregoing observation is greatest in certain important discontinuous choices and decisions, such as between two kinds of educational institutions or two modes of transportation.[8] If one assumes a complete and continuous array of varieties, from cheap and poor-quality to expensive and high-quality, then deterioration of any but the top and bottom variety will rapidly lead to a combination of exits: the quality-conscious consumers move to the higher-price, higher-quality products and the price-conscious ones go over to the lower-price, lower-quality varieties; the former will still tend to get out first

8. In Appendix D it is shown that the reversal phenomenon can occur only when there are at least three goods: the intermediate variety which is the one that deteriorates or whose price increases, another variety that is higher-priced and higher-quality, and a third with the opposite characteristics. In this constellation the less demanding consumers will exit first (toward the lower-priced, lower-quality good) when the *price* of the intermediate good increases, whereas the quality-conscious consumer will exit first (toward the higher-priced, higher-quality good) when *quality* decreases. Even though in the above example only two goods are made explicit, namely public and private school education, the required third alternative on the "other side" of the normally bought good would be present if there were a price increase for public education, namely, informal education at home. This would no doubt be the alternative chosen by many of the less demanding consumers if public schools ceased being free. Hence the presence of the reversal phenomenon cannot be ruled out in this case. A similar reasoning applies to other seemingly dichotomous choices: upon looking more closely, it is usually found that a third alternative exists; some inferior commodity can be found in case the price of the usually bought good increases.

when it is quality that declines rather than price that rises, but the latter will not be far behind.

The proposition that voice is likely to play a more important role in opposing deterioration of high-quality products than of lower-quality products can nevertheless be maintained for the case of a good with many varieties, if these varieties can be assumed not to be spread with equal *density* over the whole quality range. If only because of economies of scale, it is plausible that density is lower in the upper ranges of quality than in the lower and middle ranges. If this is so then deterioration of a product in the upper quality ranges has to be fairly substantial before the quality-conscious will exit and switch to the next better variety. Hence the scope for, and resort to, the voice option will be greatest in these ranges; it will be comparatively slight in the medium- and low-quality ranges.

This finding permits two inferences. First, it can be related to the discussion of education which suggested that the role of voice in fending off deterioration is particularly important for a number of essential services largely defining what has come to be called the "quality of life." Hence, a disconcerting, though far from unrealistic, conclusion emerges: since, in the case of these services, resistance to deterioration requires voice and since voice will be forthcoming more readily at the upper than at the lower quality ranges, the cleavage between the quality of life at the top and at the middle or lower levels will tend to become more marked. This would be particularly the case in societies with upward social mobility. In societies which inhibit passage from one social stratum to another, resort to the voice option is automatically strengthened: everyone has a strong motivation to defend the quality of life at his own station. That cleavages between the upper and lower classes tend to widen and to become more rigid in upwardly mobile societies has become increasingly obvious;

but it has not been an easy observation to make in a culture in which it had long been taken for granted that equality of opportunity combined with upward social mobility would assure both efficiency and social justice.[9]

A rather different inference results if the assumption of a progressive thinning out of varieties at the upper end of the quality scale is brought into contact with the plausible notion that a combination of exit and voice is needed for best results. If this notion is accepted, then the recuperation mechanism may rely too much on exit at the lower end of the quality scale, *but suffer from a deficiency of exit at the upper end.* An illustration of the latter proposition will be found toward the end of the book.

9. The fallacies of this belief were laid bare in Michael Young's incisive satire *The Rise of Meritocracy* (1958, Penguin Edition 1968). See also below, pp. 108–112.

5

# How Monopoly Can be Comforted
## by Competition *

The realization that a tight monopoly is preferable under certain circumstances to a looser arrangement in which competition is present comes hard to a Western economist. Nonetheless, the preceding argument compels recognition that a no-exit situation will be superior to a situation with some limited exit on two conditions:

(1) if exit is ineffective as a recuperation mechanism, but does succeed in draining from the firm or organization its more quality-conscious, alert, and potentially activist customer or members; and

(2) if voice could be made into an effective mechanism once these customers or members are securely locked in.

There are doubtless many situations in which the first condition applies—some additional examples will be given in this and later chapters. The second condition is a very large subject indeed: as was already pointed out, to develop "voice" within an organization is synonymous with the history of democratic control through the articulation and aggregation of opinions and interests.

By itself, the fact that the members or customers are locked in cannot therefore ensure that an effective volume of voice will be forthcoming. As will be argued below, one important way of bringing influence to bear on an organization is to threaten exit to the rival organization. But this threat cannot be made when there is no rival, so that voice is not only handicapped when exit is possible, but also, though in a quite different way, when it is not. Neverthe-

*In writing this chapter I inexcusably failed to refer to John Hicks's celebrated statement of 35 years ago: "The best of all monopoly profits is a quiet life." Had I remembered it, I would have been rather less critical about the economist's neglect of the "lazy monopolist." At the same time, I would have been able to express even more sharply the principal point of the chapter: On certain assumptions about the existence and intensity of voice, competition can afford an even quieter life than does monopoly.—A.O.H., September 30, 1971.

less, it is often possible to make probabilistic statements such as: considering the authority structure and responsiveness of organizations in a given society, and the general readiness of individuals and groups to assert their interests, it is likely that in this or that particular case, voice is going to do a more creditable job of maintaining efficiency when the customers or members are locked in than when some exit is available.[1]

Perhaps the best way of looking at the matter is to recognize that we face here a choice of two evils. Next to the traditional full-fledged monopoly whose dangers and possible abuses have long been exposed, attention should also be paid to those organizations whose monopoly powers are less complete, but who are characterized by sturdy, if undistinguished survival after exit of the more alert customers or members. Often there will be a real question which one of these two institutional varieties is the more unsatisfactory.

The point of view here adopted contrasts with the spirit

1. One may note an interesting symmetry here with the case of perfect competition. As pointed out in ch. 1, n. 1, the firm which produces for a perfectly competitive market finds out about its failings directly through increases in its costs rather than indirectly through customers' reactions because it cannot change either the price or the quality of its product. It will experience losses which will depend on the size of its lapse from efficiency. If the lapse is small, small too will be the losses and the firm will have an opportunity to recover. If one moves just a small step away from perfect competition, to a situation, that is, where the firm has some market power as a price- and quality-maker while demand remains very elastic, then one lands in a very different situation: a small lapse can produce a slightly deteriorated product which will lead to so large a loss of revenue that the firm immediately succumbs. It is now suggested that a similar situation may prevail at the other end of the spectrum. In some situations, a full monopoly may be preferable, from the point of view of the effectiveness of our recuperation mechanisms, to a monopoly just slightly hampered by competition. For this limited competition may result in revenue losses too small to alert management to its failings while it could weaken voice decisively by drawing away from the firm its most vocal customers. At both extremes of perfect competition and pure monopoly the recuperative mechanism may therefore work better than if only a *small step* were made from these extremes in the direction of market power and competitive structure, respectively.

that has long animated the concern over monopoly and the struggle against it. The monopolist has traditionally been expected to utilize to the utmost his ability to exploit the consumer and to maximize profits by restricting production. Public policies have been based primarily on this expectation. Even Galbraith, ordinarily so ready to repudiate the "conventional wisdom," takes this exploitative behavior to be the prime and perhaps only danger which must be guarded against. In his *American Capitalism* he merely pointed out that competition has become an unrealistic alternative to the monopolistic tendencies of advanced capitalist economies and extolled an alternative, already existing remedy, to wit, "countervailing power." But what if we have to worry, not only about the profit-maximizing exertions and exactions of the monopolist, but about his proneness to inefficiency, decay, and flabbiness? This may be, in the end, the more frequent danger: the monopolist sets a high price for his products not to amass super-profits, but because he is unable to keep his costs down; or, more typically, he allows the quality of the product or service he sells to deteriorate without gaining any pecuniary advantage in the process.[2]

In view of the spectacular nature of such phenomena as exploitation and profiteering, the nearly opposite failings which monopoly and market power allow, namely, laziness, flabbiness, and decay have come in for much less scrutiny. To find these problems recognized as public policy issues one has to look beyond the "Anglo-Saxon" world where economic thinking is usually carried on in terms of some maximizing or "taut economy" model. When, a few years ago, a prestigious French economic official put forward proposals for various public controls of business, he did single out incompetence and "abandon"

2. Compare the following remark of a student of Brazilian society: "The large Brazilian landholding is an evil not because it is inhuman and brutal, but because it is inefficient." Jacques Lambert, *Os dois Brasis* (Rio de Janeiro: INEP-Ministerio da Educação e Cultura, 1963), p. 120.

on the part of faltering corporate management as an important problem.[3]

Political power is very much like market power in that it permits the powerholder to indulge either his brutality or his flaccidity. But here again the dangers of abuse of power, of invasion of individuals' rights have—for very good reasons—stood in the center of attention, rather than those of maladministration and bureaucratic ineptitude. Accordingly, the original purpose of the now so widely discussed office of ombudsman was to help redress citizens' grievances against officials who had exceeded the constitutional limits of their power. Later, however, the institution experienced a "shift in its main purpose" which today "has become promotion of better administration," the correction of malpractices and the like.[4] This presumably means that the institution is now also used to correct and reprimand official *indolence* though it was originally devised for the purpose of stemming abuses of power on the part of overactive and overbearing officials.

Such versatility is admirable, but cannot be expected to be the rule. It would be surprising if every one of the safeguards against a monopolist's single-minded pursuit of profits turned out to do double duty as a cure of his propensity toward flabbiness and distraction. Exit-competition is a case in point. While of undoubted benefit in the case of the exploitative, profit-maximizing monopolist, the

3. François Bloch-Lainé, *Pour une réforme de l'entreprise* (Paris: Editions du Seuil, 1963), pp. 54–57, 76–77. "Anglo-Saxon" literature, particularly on trade unions, has paid some attention to the possible existence of "sleepy" or "lazy" monopolies. See, for example, Richard A. Lester, *As Unions Mature* (Princeton: Princeton University Press, 1958), pp. 56–60, and Lloyd G. Reynolds and Cynthia H. Taft, *The Evolution of Wage Structure* (New Haven: Yale University Press, 1956), p. 190. But the exploitative potential of the monopoly has always stood in the center of the discussion and it has been the exclusive motive for regulation and antitrust legislation.

4. Hing Yong Cheng, "The Emergence and Spread of the Ombudsman Institution," *The Annals*, special issue on "The Ombudsman or Citizen's Defender" (May 1968), p. 23.

presence of competition could do more harm than good when the main concern is to counteract the monopolist's tendency toward flaccidity and mediocrity. For, in that case, exit-competition could just fatally weaken voice along the lines of the preceding section, without creating a serious threat to the organization's survival. This was so for the Nigerian Railway Corporation because of the ease with which it could dip into the public treasury in case of deficit. But there are many other cases where competition does not restrain monopoly as it is supposed to, but *comforts and bolsters* it by unburdening it of its more troublesome customers. As a result, one can define an important and too little noticed type of monopoly-tyranny: a limited type, an oppression of the weak by the incompetent and an exploitation of the poor by the lazy which is the more durable and stifling as it is both *unambitious and escapable.* The contrast is stark indeed with totalitarian, expansionist tyrannies or the profit-maximizing, accumulation-minded monopolies which may have captured a disproportionate share of our attention.

In the economic sphere such "lazy" monopolies which "welcome competition" as a release from effort and criticism are frequently encountered when monopoly power rests on location and when mobility differs strongly from one group of local customers to another. If, as is likely, the mobile customers are those who are most sensitive to quality, their exit, caused by the poor performance of the local monopolist, permits him to persist in his comfortable mediocrity. This applies, for example, to small city or "ghetto" stores which lose their quality-conscious patrons to better stores elsewhere as well as to sluggish electric power utilities in developing countries whose more demanding customers will decide at some point that they can no longer afford the periodic breakdowns and will move out or install their own independent power supply.

The United States Post Office can serve as another

example of the lazy monopolist who thrives on the limited exit possibilities existing for its most fastidious and well-to-do customers. The availability of fast and reliable communications via telegraph and telephone makes the shortcomings of the mail service more tolerable; it also permits the Post Office to tyrannize the better over those of its customers who find exit to other communication modes impractical or too expensive.

Those who hold power in the lazy monopoly may actually have an interest in *creating* some limited opportunities for exit on the part of those whose voice might be uncomfortable. Here is a good illustration of the contrast between the profit-maximizing and the lazy monopolist: the former would engage, if he could, in discriminatory pricing so as to extract maximum revenue from its most avid customers, while the lazy monopolist would much rather price these customers out of the market entirely so as to be able to give up the strenuous and tiresome quest for excellence. For the most avid customers are not only willing to pay the highest prices, but are also likely to be most demanding and querulous, in case of any lowering of standards.[5]

Instances of such topsy-turvy (from the point of view of profit maximization) discrimination are not easy to document in economic life, in part perhaps because we have not looked for them very hard and in part simply because price discrimination in general is not easily practiced. But a closely analogous situation is familiar from politics. Latin American powerholders have long encouraged their political enemies and potential critics to remove themselves from the scene through voluntary exile. The

5. There is another way in which the lazy monopolist may be able to rid himself of the voice of these customers: he can extend *just to them* especially high-quality, "gold-plated" service. This would be discrimination with respect to quality rather than to price. The purpose, once again, is not to extract maximum revenue, but to buy "freedom to deteriorate."

right of asylum, so generously practiced by all Latin
American republics, could almost be considered as a "con-
spiracy in restraint of voice." An even more straightforward illustration is supplied by a Colombian law that
provided for paying former presidents as many U.S. dollars if they resided abroad as they would receive in Colombian pesos if they lived in their own country. With the
U.S. dollar being worth from five to ten pesos while the
law was in effect, the officially arranged incentive toward
exit of these potential "trouble makers" was considerable.

Even without such special incentives, exit for disgruntled or defeated politicians has always been easier in some
countries than in others. The following comparison between politics in Japan and in Latin America supplies another illustration of the corroding influence exit can have
on vigorous and constructive political processes via voice:

The isolation of Japan set rigid boundaries to the possibilities of political opposition. The absence of easy opportunities for tolerable exile was a powerful teacher of the
virtues of compromise. The Argentinean newspaper edi-
tor in danger of arrest or assassination could slip across
the river to Montevideo and still find himself a home, amid
familiar sounds and faces and familiar books, easily able
to find friends and a new job. (Nowadays, perhaps, he
would arrange a refuge in one of the mushrooming international organizations beforehand.) But to all but a tiny
fraction of Japanese only one place has ever been home.[6]

In this view, Japan gained an advantage from being a
"no-exit" polity while the ever-beckoning opportunity to
exit that was characteristic of Hispano-American societies contributed perhaps as much to the factionalism and
*personalismo* typical of their politics as the Spanish national character, the *machismo* cult, and similar conven-
tionally given reasons.

6. R. P. Dore, "Latin America and Japan Compared," in John J.
Johnson, ed., *Continuity and Change in Latin America* (Stanford:
Stanford University Press, 1964), p. 238.

# 6
## On Spatial Duopoly
## and the Dynamics of
## Two-Party Systems

The situations which have been analyzed up to now have as their point of departure a clear-cut deterioration in the performance of a firm or organization. The exit and voice options are reactions to this deterioration and, under certain conditions, will arrest and reverse it. Consumers were portrayed as being more or less sensitive to a change in quality, but they *all* experienced the change as either positive or negative. This assumption can and will now be dropped. In this respect, quality and price are once again revealed as totally different phenomena: a decline in the price of a commodity is good news for *all* consumers just as a rise in price means a loss in real income for *all*, but one and the same change in quality may make the commodity more appreciated by some consumers while others find it less to their taste than before. This is also the case, of course, for shifts in the positions of political parties and other organizations.

When firms and organizations have this possibility of changing quality in such a way as to please some while displeasing others, the question arises as to the quality which they are most likely to select. The economist's answer is that the firm will select that point on the quality scale which will maximize its profits.[1] This routine reflex does not really solve our problem, however; for if a firm both loses and gains customers by a given quality change (while costs remain unchanged) the criterion of profit maximization may not yield a unique solution at all. Or suppose that the firm is a monopolist, which does not actually lose or gain customers as it varies the quality of its

1. For simplicity's sake, it may be assumed that the quality changes in question do not affect costs.

product, but causes, through such variations, happiness and unhappiness in different groups of its customers. To make such situations determinate, it is plausible to introduce another criterion: in addition to maximizing profits, the firm will tend to minimize discontent of its customers, for the highly rational purpose of earning goodwill or reducing hostility in the community of which it is a part.[2] With this criterion in operation, the firm is in general likely to select a point in the middle of the quality range along which its profits are maximized. Suppose we have two categories of customers of a monopolistic firm, the $A$-fiends who would deplore any shift along a linear scale from quality $A$ to $B$ and the $B$-fiends who would hail it. The discontent-minimizing firm is then likely to select the midpoint between $A$ and $B$,[3] provided the intensity of discontent of both $A$- and $B$-fiends is identical. If the discontent of the $A$-fiends as quality moves away from $A$ is far stronger and more vocal than the corresponding discontent of $B$-fiends, then the firm is likely to select a quality that is considerably closer to $A$ than to $B$.

The concept of voice has just made its appearance and has made it possible to introduce determinacy into the problem of quality-selection by the firm. Instead of inter-

2. It is of course possible to equate this concern with profit maximization "in the long run."

3. If the frequency distribution of consumers' tastes has the normal shape, it is obvious that a discontent-minimizing firm will select the midpoint. Even when consumers' tastes are distributed with equal density along the $A$-$B$ scale, discontent, when assumed to be proportional to the distance between actual and desired quality, would be minimized in the same fashion. This was shown long ago for the special case in which the $A$-$B$ scale represents physical distance in a linear market (see n. 6, below). Location of the firm at some point of the scale then stands for "quality"; any change in this quality is obviously agreeable to some consumers and disagreeable to others and the cost of transportation inflicted by the firm's location on different consumers is the measure of their discontent (provided the marginal utility of money is constant). If a bimodal distribution of consumers' tastes is assumed, as was done in the text, a further condition must be imposed if it is to be concluded that the midpoint will be chosen. This is the plausible idea that discontent

preting the firm's decision to minimize discontent as a sovereign act on which it has decided out of enlightened self-interest,[4] it would have been possible and perhaps more realistic to say that, in selecting the middle of the quality range, the firm is simply responding to voice—or, rather, to customers' voices which have been assumed to be pulling the firm in opposite directions. But if voice plays so decisive a role when profit maximization provides no policy guidance to the firm, it will hardly be disregarded entirely when profit maximization points to some specific point along the quality range. In other words, the concern with voice (that is, with minimizing hostility and discontent) can be expected to qualify the concern with maximum profits. Should profit maximization conflict with

---

rises more than proportionately with deviation of the actual from the preferred quality. The discontent functions would then have the following shape:

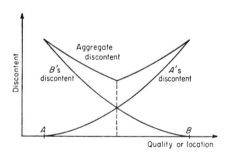

The aggregate discontent of A-fiends and B-fiends is again minimized by selecting the midpoint between A and B.

4. Or out of pure altruism, as is assumed in Otto A. Davis and Melvin Hinch, "A Mathematical Model of Policy Formulation in a Democratic Society," in J. L. Bernd, ed., *Mathematical Applications in Political Science* (Dallas: Arnold Foundation, 1966), II, 175–208. At one point in their article, the authors examine, with results similar to those in the text, how a "beneficent dictator" would minimize the citizens' "utility loss function," that is, their discontent with the policies pursued by him.

discontent-minimization, there will be some compromise or trade-off between these two objectives.

A situation in which such a conflict and trade-off are particularly likely can be constructed as follows: Suppose that, of the two categories of consumers, $A$-fiends and $B$-fiends, the former have no alternative to turn to if quality of the firm's output moves toward $B$, while $B$-fiends' demand is so highly elastic that they will desert the firm in rapidly increasing numbers as quality shifts from $B$ to $A$. In this situation a firm that single-mindedly maximizes profits will produce at point $B$ of the quality range, while one that minimizes discontent would rather produce at point $A$. At $A$, the $A$-fiends would be happy while the $B$-fiends would all have taken their business elsewhere; they might not be kindly disposed toward the firm that has disappointed them, but they have cut themselves off through exit from all or much of the influence they might exert. In any event, the fact that they found a substitute so easily makes it likely that their welfare loss was not unduly high. If the firm produces at $B$, on the contrary, the $A$-fiends would still be with it, but presumably in a state of serious and vocal discontent. In this situation, a firm that is at all sensitive to voice will withdraw some distance from the point in the quality range at which it could achieve maximum profits. Note therefore that a firm is particularly likely to be deflected from the point of maximum profits when the consumers which are made unhappy by the firm producing at that point are in the position of having "nowhere else to go." This is a result that contradicts, or at least qualifies, the conventional ideas about the "powerful consumer." His power is usually believed to originate in the fact that he can take his business elsewhere and can thus "punish" the firm which does not pay heed to his preferences, but we see now that another kind of power resides in the consumer who *cannot* take his business elsewhere and who has therefore the maximum incentive to cajole, threaten, and otherwise induce the firm to pay attention to his needs and tastes.[5]

The preceding discussion has a direct bearing on topics in economic and political thought which have a long and distinguished genealogy. Some forty years ago, Harold Hotelling published a celebrated article [6] which pioneered in a number of fields: duopoly, location theory, and the dynamics of two-party systems. His argument has been elaborated and qualified by later writers, but his basic points have not met with a direct challenge. Hotelling's principal idea can be summarized quite briefly. Customers or, in the political variant of the model, voters are assumed to be evenly distributed along a finite linear scale from *A* to *B*, or from Left to Right. Suppose that initially two firms (or two parties) have divided up this linear territory among themselves by locating at the midpoints of the left and right halves. From the social point of view, this is the ideal arrangement because it minimizes transportation costs for the consumers. In the political application of the model, the same result can be obtained: by locating at the quartiles, ideological distance between the voters and the parties and, hence, voters' discontent with the parties' platforms and policies will be minimized. Now assume that one of the two firms or parties, say, the one at the left-hand side, is allowed to shift its location without cost while the other is, or is thought to be, tied down. A profit-maximizing firm or a vote-maximizing party is

5. As long as quality change was defined as a deterioration that is felt as such by *all* consumers, exit and voice were pushing the firm in the same direction. If the firm mends its ways, the ensuing recovery will therefore be a "joint product" of exit and voice and it will be difficult to disentangle and evaluate the respective contributions of each. When quality change means improvement for some and deterioration for others, the comparative strength of the two mechanisms is more easily tested because they may work, as just explained, in opposite directions. I return to this point at the end of the present chapter.

6. "Stability in Competition," *Economic Journal,* 39:41–57 (1929).

under these conditions likely to move toward the right. The reason is that as long as it makes a point of staying to the left of the tied-down firm it retains a firm hold on its far-left customers or voters, while it can snatch new customers and voters away from the right-wing firm or party by advancing into its territory. Two important conclusions follow: (1) under the assumed conditions of duopoly there will be a tendency for the two firms to move toward the middle of the scale; (2) profit- or vote-maximizing behavior leads in this fashion to socially undesirable results since goods will be made available to consumers at higher total costs (if transportation costs borne by the consumer are counted) than would obtain if the firms had remained anchored at the quartiles. In a similar way it can be argued that it is probable, but socially undesirable, for parties in a two-party system to move ever closer together.[7]

The success which this elegant model has had, particularly among political scientists, is matched only by its

7. There is one important difference: after the political contest between the two parties is decided, the winning party takes over the government for the whole country while in the case of duopoly, the two firms permanently share the market among themselves. Thus, by locating at the quartiles, the parties would minimize the public's discontent with their positions and their policies, but not with those of the government that is the outcome of the struggle between the two parties. It can be argued, however, that a two-party system implies a preference for a risky but meaningful over a meaningless choice. Put somewhat differently, the average citizen may well prefer a situation in which a party with which he identifies closely has an even chance of beating one he sharply disagrees with, over a situation in which power is always held by a middle-of-the-road party which he neither likes nor dislikes strongly. This point is overlooked by Davis and Hinch, who view the possible location of the two candidates at the quartiles as a result of a nomination process in the course of which each party's nominee is selected exclusively by the members of that party. This is quite realistic in terms of the institutions of American democracy. But the result is not necessarily objectionable from the point of view of the community as a whole, as would seem to be implied by the Davis-Hinch analysis, which sets up the hypothetical policies pursued by a "beneficent dictator" as some sort of optimal solution. See n. 4, above.

failure to predict correctly the actual course of events—a fine illustration of the Streeten-Kuhn maxim that a model is never defeated by facts, however damaging, but only by another model.[8] Not that the model was left entirely untouched. When, in the wake of the Depression and the New Deal, the Democratic and Republican parties moved farther apart ideologically, an attempt was made to reconcile the model with these events. Advantage was taken of the fact that the results of the model depended critically —as had already been pointed out by Hotelling [9]—on the assumption of zero elasticity of demand throughout the linear market. With that assumption, consumers continue to buy the product from the nearest store no matter how far is "nearest" and citizens similarly go on voting for the party closest to them. If demand is elastic, on the other hand, a firm or party would lose customers or voters at its own end of the market as it moved toward the center and this loss of business or votes would at least restrain the socially undesirable clustering tendency of the original model.[10]

The pendulum of the facts swung back in the other direction in the fifties, with the soporific calm of the Eisenhower years and the somewhat premature announcement on the part of prominent scholars that ideology was dead.

8. Paul Streeten formulated this maxim in a letter to the author. The idea is persuasively developed in Thomas S. Kuhn's *The Structure of Scientific Revolutions* (Chicago: University of Chicago Press, 1962).

9. "Stability in Competition," p. 56.

10. Demand was assumed to be elastic throughout the linear market or to attain positive elasticity beyond a given range of transportation costs in the articles of Arthur Smithies ("Optimum Location in Spatial Competition," *Journal of Political Economy*, 49:423–439 [1941]) and of A. P. Lerner and H. W. Singer ("Some Notes on Duopoly and Spatial Competition," *Journal of Political Economy*, 45:145–186 [1939]), respectively. Smithies specifically presented his modification of the Hotelling model as a way of accounting for the strengthening of the ideological stances of the Democratic and Republican parties in the thirties, in contrast to the dilution of ideologies in the late twenties when Hotelling wrote.

In this atmosphere the Hotelling model was touched up once again. In a well-known work, Anthony Downs questioned the realism of the Hotelling assumption that voters are evenly distributed along the ideological spectrum, between the Left and Right.[11] If the frequency distribution of the voters along this scale has one peak toward the middle (the "middle-of-the-road") and tapers off toward both extremes, then Hotelling's clustering tendency will obviously assert itself once again. (It should be remarked that, in these conditions, the tendency would not cause the sort of social loss that it implies on the assumption of even distribution.) Thus Downs rehabilitated the Hotelling thesis, not by questioning the assumption of elastic demand through which the thesis had been qualified—to the contrary, he fully endorsed that qualification—but by counterbalancing elastic demand with the assumption of a more or less "normal" frequency distribution of the voters from Left to Right.[12]

As soon as the Hotelling model had been thus refurbished by Downs, its power to explain reality was again cast into doubt by the undisciplined vagaries of history. The selection by the Republican party of Goldwater in 1964 and, to a lesser extent, of Nixon in 1968 testified to the extreme reluctance of at least one party to conform to the Hotelling-Downs scenario. In general, evidence was increasing that the two parties were fairly consistently on opposite sides of many important issues.[13]

The concept of voice permits a more fundamental re-

11. *An Economic Theory of Democracy* (New York: Harper and Brothers, 1956), ch. 8.
12. Downs devoted much space to examining the results of other types of frequency distributions on two-party and multi-party systems. But in his discussion of two-party systems, he stresses the tendencies toward convergence and ambiguity of party positions and thus essentially bolstered the original Hotelling findings.
13. See S. M. Lipset, *Revolution and Counter-Revolution: Change and Resistance in Social Structures* (New York: Basic Books, 1968), p. 398, and literature there quoted (n. 27).

vision of the Hotelling model than was achieved in the thirties by introducing elastic demand. The fact is that Hotelling's original assumption of inelastic demand is perfectly realistic under conditions of a duopoly selling an essential good and of a well-established two-party system. It was not this assumption that was wrong or unrealistic, *but the inference that the "captive" consumer (or voter) who has "nowhere else to go" is the epitome of powerlessness.* True, he cannot exit to the other firm or party and in this way bring pressure on his own firm or party to improve its performance, but just because of that he, unlike the consumer or voter who can exit, will be maximally motivated to bring all sorts of potential influence into play so as to keep the firm or the party from doing things that are highly obnoxious to him. Hotelling's clustering tendency can therefore be countered and restrained not by substituting elastic for inelastic demand in his model, but by realizing that inelastic demand at the extremes of the linear market can spell considerable influence *via voice.*

As already outlined, voice will force the firm or the party to trade its profit-making or vote-getting objectives to some extent against the discontent-reducing objective. Such a trade-off becomes even more likely when the inevitable uncertainty about prospective sales or votes is taken into account. In other words, a party which is beleaguered by protests from disgruntled members because they dislike proposed "wishy-washy" platforms or policies will often be tempted to give in to these voices because they are very real here and now, while the benefits that are to accrue from wishy-washiness are highly conjectural.

The general conditions for the use of voice have been discussed in Chapter 2. With respect to the subject now under discussion, the matter can perhaps best be formulated as follows: for voice to function properly it is necessary that individuals possess reserves of political influence which they can bring into play when they are sufficiently aroused. That this is generally so—that, in other words, there is considerable slack in political systems—is well recognized. "Nearly every citizen in the community has access to unused political resources" writes Robert Dahl.[14]

Clearly, Hotelling's concern about the social losses that might be caused by the clustering tendency was excessive. Those who are made unhappy by the party's wishy-washy position can influence the party through a mechanism that is none the less powerful for operating outside the market. On the other hand, there can be no guarantee that the voice mechanism will bring the party exactly back to the somewhat problematical "social optimum" which, in analogy to Hotelling's treatment of the location problem, can be defined as the point at which the sum of the ideological distances between the party and its clients is minimized. The influence of those who have nowhere else to go may well make the party overshoot that point, with disastrous consequences for its vote-gathering objectives. This was essentially what happened to the Republican party in 1964 with the selection of Goldwater as its presidential nominee.

Hardly ever was a hypothesis so cruelly contradicted by the facts as were the predictions of the Hotelling-Downs theory by the Goldwater nomination. Nevertheless, not even this event led to an outright questioning of the theory. In a searching article, three political scientists looked for the reasons for which the Republican party had so clearly failed to act as the vote-maximizer on that occasion.[15] They came close to the correct answer by focusing on the right-wing of the party and by showing that this element was far more activist than the middle-of-the-

14. *Who Governs?* (New Haven: Yale University Press, 1961), p. 309.
15. P. E. Converse, A. R. Clausen, and W. E. Miller, "Election Myths and Reality: The 1964 Election," *American Political Science Review*, 59:321–336 (June 1965).

roaders. The writing of letters to public officials or to newspapers and magazines was investigated as a particular type of intense political activity and it was shown that indeed this activity was engaged in to a wholly disproportionate extent by those right-wing Republicans who "had nowhere else to go." But the authors use these most interesting data primarily to explain the *misperceptions* of the Republican party and of their nominee with respect to the chances for victory, instead of drawing the following, much more basic conclusion: in a two-party system a party will not necessarily behave as the Hotelling-Downs vote-maximizer because those "who have nowhere else to go" are not powerless but influential.[16]

This power of those who have nowhere else to go in a two-party system has come to light in a different form with the Democratic defeat in the 1968 elections. The mobilization of the indifferent voters and the winning over of the undecided ones was seen to depend to a considerable extent on the enthusiasm which each of the parties can inspire among activist party workers and volunteers. Since the activists are far from being middle-of-the-roaders, their enthusiasm can be dampened by a party's moving to an excessively middle-of-the-road position. Hence the adoption of a platform which is designed to gain votes at the center can be counter-productive: it may damage rather than shore up the party's fortunes at the polls. With this mechanism the voice of those who have nowhere to go actually works "through the market" as it imposes

16. In the last paragraph of the article, something of this conclusion is in fact suggested by the authors: "The intense levels of political motivation which underlie the letter-writing of the ultra-conservative wing are part and parcel of the ingredients which led to a Republican convention delegation so markedly discrepant from either the rank-and-file of the Party or its customary leadership." But apart from this statement, the whole emphasis of the article is on the misperception of the party, rather than on the misjudgment of those who expect the party to conform to the Hotelling-Downs model.

decreasing and at some point negative returns on a move of the party to the center. It is as though those who are located at the end of a linear market were in charge of advertising the firm's products to those in the middle; naturally their advertising zeal is likely to go down as the firm moves its site farther and farther away from them.

In this sort of constellation traditional analysis would have no difficulty recognizing the limitations of the Hotelling-Downs model. The same goes for another qualification of the model which has already been mentioned: when sufficiently antagonized and outraged, the supposedly captive members may either "sit this one out" or even secede from the party and set up their own movement, however futile a gesture this may be. Here demand at the extreme would turn out to be elastic after all rather than totally inelastic and traditional concepts would account well enough for what is happening.[17] But the crux of the matter can now be sharply stated. These situations in which the supposedly powerless voters at the extreme manage to inflict actual vote losses on the party if it moves too far to the center are only special manifestations of the general influence and power that come with "having nowhere to go." In other words, that power exists and that influence will be brought to bear even without such direct and measurable effects on the party's vote (or the firm's profits). There are *a great many ways* in which customers, voters, and party members can impress their unhappiness on a firm or a party and make their managers highly uncom-

17. In line with the analyses of Lerner, Singer, and Smithies, in the articles cited in n. 10, above, Downs speaks in this connection of the "influence type of party" or of "blackmail parties" (*Economic Theory of Democracy*, pp. 131–132). Insofar as abstention is concerned, recent research shows that by far the principal influence on voter turnout has been the ease or cumbersomeness of the registration procedure rather than voter commitment to, or alienation from, individual candidates. See Stanley Kelley, Jr., R. E. Ayres, and W. G. Bowen, "Registration and Voting: Putting First Things First," *American Political Science Review*, 61:359–379 (June 1967).

fortable; only a few of these ways, and not necessarily the most important ones, will result in a loss of sales or votes, rather than in, say, loss of sleep by the managers.[18]

The situation which has been discussed here invites one further speculation. It has previously been pointed out that different organizations are differentially sensitive to voice and exit and that the optimal mix of voice and exit will therefore differ from one type of organization to another. For example, state enterprise which in case of a cash deficit due to revenue losses knows it can rely on the treasury is likely to be far more sensitive, at least up to a point, to voice (protests of consumers, appeals to higher authorities to replace existing management, and so forth) than to exit. This differential responsiveness has interesting consequences when the change in quality that gives rise to consumer reaction is felt as deterioration by some consumers while others sense the change as an improvement. Assume in addition that, as the quality moves in one direction, the organization exposes itself primarily to exit because the members antagonized by that move have an alternative organization to join while a move in the opposite direction will primarily activate voice of the antagonized, but "captive," consumers. It is then possible to predict the "quality path" of the firm or organization. Suppose small quality changes in the organization's performance occur constantly as a result of random events. If the organization responds more to voice than to exit, it is much more likely to correct deviations from normal quality that are obnoxious to its "captive" consumers; whereas deviations from quality that lead to exit of its noncaptive, exit-prone consumers would tend to go uncorrected for a considerable time.

Insofar as this situation approximates reality, it provides a rationale for the radicalization of political move-

18. See also Appendix A, last paragraph.

ment. The day-to-day policies of these movements tend to be influenced—specially when they are out of power—by their present activist members rather than by the preoccupation with losing the favor of all members and voters. Hence a shift toward the center which antagonizes the captive but activist members is likely to be resisted more strenuously than a radical shift, even though the latter might lead to exit of the noncaptive members and voters. One could conjecture that radicalization of political movements predicted by this model would assert itself the more strongly the longer the interval between elections; for electoral considerations can be expected to exert some restraining influence on the power of the captive party members. But this whole matter is further complicated by the phenomenon of organizational *loyalty*.

# 7

# A Theory
# of Loyalty

As was pointed out in earlier chapters, the presence of the exit option can sharply reduce the probability that the voice option will be taken up widely and effectively. Exit was shown to drive out voice, in other words, and it began to look as though voice is likely to play an important role in organizations only on condition that exit is virtually ruled out. In a large number of organizations one of the two mechanisms is in fact wholly dominant: on the one hand, there is competitive business enterprise where performance maintenance relies heavily on exit and very little on voice; on the other, exit is ordinarily unthinkable, though not always wholly impossible, from such primordial human groupings as family, tribe, church, and state. The principal way for the individual member to register his dissatisfaction with the way things are going in these organizations is normally to make his voice heard in some fashion.[1]

As an aside, it is worth noting that, with exit either impossible or unthinkable, provision is generally made in these organizations for expelling or excommunicating the individual member in certain circumstances. Expulsion can be interpreted as an instrument—one of many—which "management" uses in these organizations to restrict resort to voice by members; a higher authority can then in turn restrict the powers of management by prohibiting expulsion, as is for example done to protect con-

---

1. There is no intention here to associate absence of exit with "primitiveness." Edmund Leach has noted that many so-called primitive tribes are far from being closed societies. In his classic study *Political Systems of Highland Burma* (1954) he traced in detail the way in which members of one social system (*gumsha*) will periodically move to another (*gumlao*) and back again. Exit may be more effectively ruled out in a so-called advanced open society than among the tribes studied by Leach.

sumers when a public service is supplied in conditions of monopoly. But when exit is a wide-open option and voice is largely nonexistent, as in the relations between a firm and its customers in competitive markets, expulsion of a member or customer is a pointless affair and does not need to be specifically prohibited. One way of catching that somewhat rare bird, an organization where exit and voice both hold important roles, may be to look for groupings from which members can both exit and be expelled. Political parties and voluntary associations in general are excellent examples.

## The Activation of Voice as a Function of Loyalty

A more solid understanding of the conditions favoring coexistence of exit and voice is gained by introducing the concept of *loyalty*. Clearly the presence of loyalty makes exit less likely, but does it, by the same token, give more scope to voice?

That the answer is in the positive can be made plausible by referring to the earlier discussion of voice. In Chapter 3 two principal determinants of the readiness to resort to voice when exit is possible were shown to be:

(1) the extent to which customer-members are willing to trade off the certainty of exit against the uncertainties of an improvement in the deteriorated product; and

(2) the estimate customer-members have of their ability to influence the organization.

Now the first factor is clearly related to that special attachment to an organization known as loyalty. Thus, even with a given estimate of one's influence, the likelihood of voice increases with the degree of loyalty. In addition, the two factors are far from independent. A member with a considerable attachment to a product or organization will often search for ways to make himself influential,

especially when the organization moves in what he be-
lieves is the wrong direction; conversely, a member who
wields (or thinks he wields) considerable power in an
organization and is therefore convinced that he can get it
"back on the track" is likely to develop a strong affection
for the organization in which he is powerful.[2]

As a rule, then, loyalty holds exit at bay and activates
voice. It is true that, in the face of discontent with the
way things are going in an organization, an individual
member can remain loyal without being influential himself, but hardly without the expectation that *someone* will
act or *something* will happen to improve matters. That
paradigm of loyalty, "our country, right or wrong," surely
makes no sense whatever if it were expected that "our"
country were to continue forever to do nothing but wrong.
Implicit in that phrase is the expectation that "our" country can be moved again in the right direction after doing
some wrong—after all, it was preceded in Decatur's toast
by "Our country! In her intercourse with foreign nations,
may she always be in the right!" The possibility of influence is in fact cleverly intimated in the saying by the use
of the possessive "our." This intimation of some influence
and the expectation that, over a period of time, the right
turns will more than balance the wrong ones, profoundly
distinguishes loyalty from faith. A glance at Kierke-
gaard's celebrated interpretation of Abraham's setting
out to sacrifice Isaac makes one realize that, in comparison

2. In terms of figure 3 of Appendix B, a person whose influence
(that is, the likelihood that he will be able to achieve full quality
recuperation) is correctly expressed by a point as high as $V_3$ will
be willing to trade off the certainty of the competing product against
even a little hope of recuperation for the traditional product. Thus
he will choose voice. He who has little influence and knows it, on the
other hand, is not likely to take kindly to such a trade-off. If he is to
opt for voice rather than exit, he will normally require the certain
availability of the competing product to be matched by the near-cer-
tainty of recuperation for the traditional variety.

to that act of pure faith, the most loyalist behavior retains an enormous dose of reasoned calculation.

*When is loyalty functional?*

The importance of loyalty from our point of view is that it can neutralize within certain limits the tendency of the most quality-conscious customers or members to be the first to exit. As has been shown in Chapter 4, this tendency deprives the faltering firm or organization of those who could best help it fight its shortcomings and its difficulties. As a result of loyalty, these potentially most influential customers and members will stay on longer than they would ordinarily, in the hope or, rather, reasoned expectation that improvement or reform can be achieved "from within." Thus loyalty, far from being irrational, can serve the socially useful purpose of preventing deterioration from becoming cumulative, as it so often does when there is no barrier to exit.

As just explained, the barrier to exit constituted by loyalty is of finite height—it can be compared to such barriers as protective tariffs. As infant industry tariffs have been justified by the need to give local industry a chance to become efficient, so a measure of loyalty to a firm or organization has the function of giving that firm or organization a chance to recuperate from a lapse in efficiency. Specific institutional barriers to exit can often be justified on the ground that they serve to stimulate voice in deteriorating, yet recuperable organizations which would be prematurely destroyed through free exit. This seems the most valid, though often not directly intended, reason for the complication of divorce procedures and for the expenditure of time, money, and nerves that they necessitate. Similarly the American labor law sets up a fairly complex and time-consuming procedure for one trade union to take over from another as the sole certified bargaining agent at the plant level. Consequently, when workers are dissatisfied with the services of a union, they cannot switch easily and rapidly to another and are that much more likely to make an effort at revitalizing the union with which they are affiliated.

The previous discussion of the alternative between exit and voice makes it possible to say something about the conditions under which specific institutional barriers to exit, or, in their absence, the generalized, informal barrier of loyalty are particularly desirable or "functional." It was shown, for one, that in the choice between voice and exit, voice will often lose out, not necessarily because it would be less effective than exit, but because its effectiveness depends on the *discovery* of *new* ways of exerting influence and pressure toward recovery. However "easy" such a discovery may look in retrospect the chances for it are likely to be heavily discounted in *ex ante* estimates, for creativity always comes as a surprise. Loyalty then helps to redress the balance by raising the cost of exit. It thereby pushes men into the alternative, creativity-requiring course of action from which they would normally recoil and performs a function similar to the underestimate of the prospective task's difficulties. I have elsewhere described how such underestimates can act as a beneficial "Hiding Hand" in just this manner.[3] Loyalty or specific institutional barriers to exit are therefore particularly functional whenever the effective use of voice requires a great deal of social inventiveness while exit is an available, yet not wholly effective, option.

Secondly, the usefulness of loyalty depends on the closeness of the available substitute. When the outputs of two competing organizations are miles apart with respect to price or quality, there is much scope for voice to come into

3. *Development Projects Observed* (Washington: Brookings Institution, 1967), ch. 1.

play in the course of progressive deterioration of one of them before exit will assume massive proportions. Thus, loyalty is hardly needed here, whereas its role as a barrier to exit can be constructive when organizations are close substitutes so that a small deterioration of one of them will send customer-members scurrying to the other. This conclusion is a little unexpected. Expressed as a paradox, it asserts that loyalty is at its most functional when it looks most irrational, when loyalty means strong attachment to an organization that does not seem to warrant such attachment because it is so much like another one that is also available. Such seemingly irrational loyalties are often encountered, for example, in relation to clubs, football teams, and political parties. Even though it was argued in Chapter 6 that parties in a two-party system are less likely to move toward and resemble each other than has sometimes been predicted, the tendency does assert itself on occasion. The more this is so the more irrational and outright silly does stubborn party loyalty look; yet that is precisely when it is most useful. Loyalty to one's country, on the other hand, is something we could do without, since countries can ordinarily be considered to be well-differentiated products. Only as countries start to resemble each other because of the advances in communication and all-round modernization will the danger of premature and excessive exits arise, the "brain drain" being a current example. At that point, a measure of loyalty will stand us in good stead. Also, there are some countries that resemble each other a good deal because they share a common history, language, and culture; here again loyalty is needed more than in countries that stand more starkly alone as was precisely implied by the comparison between Latin America and Japan, which was cited above (Chapter 5).

Finally, what was said in Chapter 4 about the danger of losing influential customers when a higher-quality, higher-price product is available "nearby," points to another conclusion on the comparative need for loyalty. If organizations can be ranked along a single scale in order of quality, prestige, or some other desirable characteristic, then those at the densely occupied lower end of the scale will need loyalty and cohesive ideology to a greater extent than those at the top. There is much evidence that this need is being appreciated both among various "left behind" groups of American society and, in the international arena, among the countries of the Third World. In the next chapter it will be shown that the most prestigious organizations and groups might, to the contrary, benefit from a decline in the level of loyalty they command.

### The loyalist's threat of exit

Loyalty is a key concept in the battle between exit and voice not only because, as a result of it, members may be locked into their organizations a little longer and thus use the voice option with greater determination and resourcefulness than would otherwise be the case. It is helpful also because it implies the possibility of disloyalty, that is, exit. Just as it would be impossible to be good in a world without evil, so it makes no sense to speak of being loyal to a firm, a party, or an organization with an unbreakable monopoly. While loyalty postpones exit its very existence is predicated on the possibility of exit. That even the most loyal member can exit is often an important part of his bargaining power vis-à-vis the organization. The chances for voice to function effectively as a recuperation mechanism are appreciably strengthened if voice is backed up by the *threat of exit,* whether it is made openly or whether the possibility of exit is merely well understood to be an element in the situation by all concerned.

In the absence of feelings of loyalty, exit per se is essentially costless, except for the cost of gathering information about alternative products and organizations. Also, when loyalty is not present, the individual member is likely to have a low estimate of his influence on the organization, as already explained. Hence, the decision to exit will be taken and carried out in silence. The threat of exit will typically be made by the loyalist—that is, by the member who cares—who leaves no stone unturned before he resigns himself to the painful decision to withdraw or switch.

The relationship between voice and exit has now become more complex. So far it has been shown how easy availability of the exit option makes the recourse to voice less likely. Now it appears that the *effectiveness* of the voice mechanism is strengthened by the possibility of exit. The willingness to develop and use the voice mechanism is reduced by exit, but the ability to use it with effect is increased by it. Fortunately, the contradiction is not insoluble. Together, the two propositions merely spell out the conditions under which voice (a) will be resorted to and (b) bids fair to be effective: there should be the possibility of exit, but exit should not be too easy or too attractive as soon as deterioration of one's own organization sets in.

The correctness of this proposition can be illustrated by the extent to which parties are responsive to the voice of the membership. The parties of totalitarian one-party systems have been notoriously unresponsive—as have been the parties of multi-party systems. In the former case, the absence of the possibility of either voice or exit spelled absolute control of the party machinery by whatever leadership dominated the party. But in the second case, with both exit and voice freely available, internal democracy does not get much of a chance to develop either because, with many parties in the field, members will usually find it tempting to go over to some other party in case of disagreement. Thus they will not fight for "change from within." In this connection it may be significant that Michels's "Iron Law of Oligarchy" according to which all parties (and other large-scale organizations) are invariably ruled by self-serving oligarchies was based on first-hand acquaintance primarily with the multi-party systems of Continental Western Europe. The best possible arrangement for the development of party responsiveness to the feelings of members may then be a system of just a very few parties, whose distance from each other is wide, but not unbridgeable. In this situation, exit remains possible, but the decision to exit will not be taken lightheartedly. Hence voice will be a frequent reaction to discontent with the way things are going and members will fight to make their voice effective. This prediction of our theory is confirmed by the lively internal struggles characteristic of parties in existing two-party systems, however far they may be from being truly democratic. Even in parties in nontotalitarian almost-one-party systems, as for example the Congress party of India and the PRI (Partido Revolucionario Institucional) of Mexico, voice has been more in evidence than in many of the often highly authoritarian or oligarchic parties of multi-party systems.*

In two-party systems, exit can happen not only as a re-

* A related point of considerable importance is suggested to me by the recent article of Michael Walzer, "Corporate Authority and Civil Disobedience," *Dissent* (September–October 1969), pp. 396–406. The strict democratic controls to which supreme political authority is subjected in Western democracies are contrasted in the article with the frequently total absence of such controls in corporate bodies functioning within these same states. As the author shows, this absence or feebleness of voice in most commercial, industrial, professional, educational, and religious organizations is often justified by the argument that "if [their members] don't like it where they are, they can leave" (p. 397), something they cannot do in relation to the state itself. Walzer argues strongly that this argument is a poor excuse which should not be allowed to stand in the way of democratization; but as a matter of positive political science, it is useful to note that the greater the opportunities for exit, the easier it appears to be for organizations to resist, evade, and postpone the introduction of internal democracy even though they function in a democratic environment.

sult of a member or group of members of one party going over to the other, but because it is always possible to launch a third party. Hence, if voice is to be given a fair try by the members, such launching must not be too easy —a condition that is usually fulfilled by the very existence and tradition of the two-party system, as well as by the institutional obstacles ordinarily placed in the way of third parties. On the other hand, if voice is to be at its most effective, the threat of exit must be credible, particularly when it most counts. In American presidential politics this set of conditions for maximizing the effectiveness of voice means that a group of party members should be able to stay within the party up to the nominating convention and still be able to form a third party between the end of the convention and election time. If exit is made too difficult by requiring the group to qualify as a party at a date *prior* to the convention, the dissenting group must either exit before the convention or go to the convention without being able to make an effective threat of exit. More stringent conditions for exit fail here to strengthen voice; rather they make for either premature exit or for less effective voice. The point is well put by Alexander Bickel:

The characteristic American third party . . . consists of a group of people who have tried to exert influence within one of the major parties, have failed, and later decide to work on the outside. States in which there is an early qualifying date tend to force such groups to forego major-party primary and other prenomination activity and organize separately, early in an election year. For if they do not they lose all opportunity for action as a third party later.[4]

The author adds that this is counterproductive from the point of view of the two-party system; the same judgment can be made from the point of view of achieving

4. Alexander M. Bickel, "Is Electoral Reform the Answer?" *Commentary* (December 1968), p. 51.

party responsiveness to its members through the most effective mix of voice and exit.

Two conclusions stand out from this discussion: (1) the detail of institutional design can be of considerable importance for the balance of exit and voice; (2) this balance, in turn, can help account for the varying extent of internal democracy in organizations.

### Boycott

Boycott is another phenomenon on the border line between voice and exit, just like the threat of exit. Through boycott, exit is actually consummated rather than just threatened; but it is undertaken for the specific and explicit purpose of achieving a change of policy on the part of the boycotted organization and is therefore a true hybrid of the two mechanisms. The threat of exit as an instrument of voice is here replaced by its mirror image, the promise of re-entry: for it is understood that the member-customer will return to the fold in case certain conditions which have led to the boycott are remedied.

Boycott is often a weapon of customers who do not have, at least at the time of the boycott, an alternative source of supply for the goods or services they are ordinarily buying from the boycotted firm or organization, but who can do temporarily without them. It is thus a temporary exit without corresponding entry elsewhere and is costly to both sides, much like a strike. In this respect also it combines characteristics of exit, which causes losses to the firm or organization, with those of voice, which is costly in time and money for the member-customers.

### Elements for a model of loyalist behavior

It may be helpful to set up a more formal model of what happens when choice between two competing goods or organizations is affected by loyalty. For the purpose of this inquiry, it will be assumed once again that the normally bought product or the organization to which one belongs begins to deteriorate. The focus will now be on organizations and their policies, rather than on firms and their products. Quality deterioration must therefore be redefined in subjective terms: from the member's viewpoint, it is equivalent to increasing disagreement with the organization's policies.

In figure 1 the horizontal axis measures quality of an

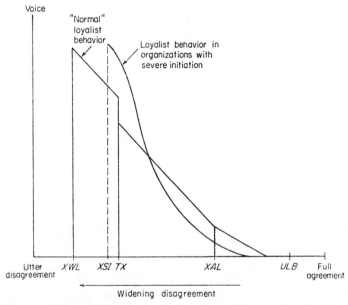

Figure 1. Loyalist behavior in the face of increasing disagreement with an organization

organization which is moving from the point where the member finds himself in complete agreement with its policies to the point of total disagreement. The vertical axis measures the amount of effective voice that is forthcoming in response to various degrees of disagreement.

At some point in the process of the organization's heading in the "wrong" direction, members will begin attempts to use their influence to correct and reverse the process, and these attempts will become stronger as disagreement widens. There comes a point in this process at which exit would take place in the absence of loyalty ($XAL$—point of eXit in the Absence of Loyalty). Loyalty now acts as a brake on the decision to exit. The *loyal* member does *not* exit, *but something happens to him:* he begins to be acutely unhappy about continuing as a member, contracts qualms or *Bauchschmerzen* (bellyaches) as the phrase went among German Communist party members dissatisfied with the party line. Normally he will make stronger attempts than hitherto to change the line and will intensify the use of voice in its various forms for this purpose; hence we show a kink in the voice function at this point, and a steeper slope after it. Then, as disagreement widens further, the member will have thoughts of exit and threaten it ($TX$—point of Threat of eXit) if that action can be at all expected to enhance the effectiveness of voice. The threat of exit means a discontinuous increase in the amount of voice that is forthcoming; this explains the vertical slope of the voice function at this point. Finally, loyalty reaches its breaking point and exit ensues (at point $XWL$—point of eXit With Loyalty). The strength of the grip which loyalty has on the customer or member can be measured either by the distance between $XAL$ and $TX$ or by that between $XAL$ and $XWL$. These two distances define two different varieties of loyalty. The former represents loyalty with no thought of exit—in many basic organizations, exit is normally entirely outside the horizon of the member, even though he may be quite unhappy about his condition as member. The distance between $XAL$ and $XWL$ represents a more inclusive concept of loyalist behavior. The distance $TX$-$XWL$ represents the portion of the process of deterioration during which the member thinks about exit and is liable to use the threat of exit for the purpose of changing the policies of the organization. This threat being in some situations a particularly potent weapon, the total volume of effective voice that is generated in the course of the process of deterioration may be more closely related to that distance than to the total stretch of loyalist behavior *(XAL-XWL)*.

With the help of this model, speculation about the loyalist's behavior can be carried a little further. Suppose he has exited (exit from a product means ordinarily "entry" into a competing product, whereas exit from an organization can mean simply passage from the set of members to the set of nonmembers) and the product or organization he has left achieves recovery: At what point of the organization's "road back" will he re-enter? It seems quite unlikely that he will do so as soon as recovery reaches point *XWL* at which he exited. Just because he suffered between *XAL* and *XWL* he will now wait *at least* until the product or the organization has returned to point *XAL* at which previously he began to have qualms. He may very well require higher quality as an extra margin of insurance that renewed slippage will not immediately saddle him with *Bauchschmerzen* once again; in many cases, of course, the whole process may have left behind such scars that re-entry is altogether inconceivable. Thus the points of exit and re-entry will be far from identical; the distance between them, if it could be measured, would yield another way of measuring the strength of loyalty for different products and organizations.

If progressive deterioration and then improvement of quality in the above model is replaced by successive declines and then increases in the prices of assets, loyalist behavior is seen to be akin to that of the naïve, small, odd-lot investor who typically sells stocks cheap to stop his losses and buys back dear after stock values have risen considerably beyond those at which they were sold. Unlike such investors, however, the loyalist is not necessarily a "sucker"; his sticking with the deteriorating product or organization should have as counterpart an increase in the chances of their recovery. It is only if such recovery fails to occur that he looks like, and turns out to be, a sucker. But in that case he has lost the bet on recovery that is implicit in loyalist behavior.

An observation of interest to the economist: loyalist behavior as sketched out here leads to a breakup of the traditional demand curve which establishes a one-to-one relationship between price (or quality) and quantity bought into two distinct curves. When a loyalty-commanding product first deteriorates and then improves, there will be one demand schedule for the downward movement in quality, with low demand elasticities at the beginning and high ones eventually as intolerable deterioration finally does lead to exit of the loyalists, and quite another one as quality recovers. During the improvement phase, elasticities will be low in the low-quality ranges and will only eventually become higher as improvement is confirmed.[5]

5. This proposition is easily diagrammed. The figure below shows quantity bought on the horizontal axis and quality (deterioration) on the vertical axis. Suppose quality first stands at $Q_1$, then de-

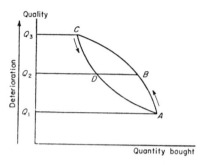

teriorates gradually to $Q_3$ and thereafter recovers slowly back to $Q_1$. Curve $ABC$ then shows the demand schedule for the deterioration phase while curve $CDA$ portrays demand for the recovery phase. Depending on the phase of the decline-recovery cycle, demand for quality $Q_2$ is either $Q_2B$ or $Q_2D$.

Demand is of course always likely to be a function not only of current, but to some extent also of previous, quality because of inertia and lags in perception. Loyalty strongly reinforces this influence of past performance of the firm or organization on present behavior of the customers or members.

These remarks make it tempting to introduce the concept of *unconscious* loyalist behavior. A situation similar to the one in which the points of exit and of re-entry do not coincide has been described by psychologists. If, say, the likeness of a cat is made to change gradually into that of a dog through a succession of images shown to a subject and if later the same series is shown in reverse order, the eye behaves as though it were "loyal" to whatever figure it started with: when the sequence is shown in the cat to dog direction, a majority of images will be labeled "cat," and vice versa.[6] To this extent then, the general difficulties of recognizing change are a breeding ground for unconscious loyalist behavior in case of deterioration, as well as for prolonged reluctance toward entry or re-entry in case the organization improves.[7] Since unconscious loyalist behavior is by definition free from felt discontent, it will not lead to voice. This behavior whose onset is marked by point

6. K. R. L. Hall, "Perceiving and Naming a Series of Figures," *Quarterly Journal of Experimental Psychology*, 2:153–162 (1950). Similar results have been obtained in experiments designed to investigate how diverse bits and pieces of information are combined and integrated. When, for example, several personality trait adjectives are read to the subjects of the experiment, the over-all judgment about the person described by the adjectives depends on the order in which the adjectives have been named, with the earlier-named ones apparently receiving a higher weight. For instance, the sequence "intelligent, prudent, moody, self-centered" produces a better over-all impression than the reverse sequence. This phenomenon is known as "primacy effect." See Norman H. Anderson, "Primacy Effects in Personality Impression Formation," *Journal of Social Psychology*, 2:1–9 (June 1965), and literature there noted.

7. Robert Jervis, "Hypotheses on Misperception," *World Politics*, 20:439–453 (April 1968), and Albert O. Hirschman, "Underdevelopment, Obstacles to the Perception of Change, and Leadership," *Daedalus* (Summer 1968), pp. 925–936.

*ULB* (*Un*conscious *Loyal Behavior*) is loyalist only from the point of view of an outside observer who feels that voice- or exit-justifying deterioration has indeed set in. The member is simply unaware of the degree of deterioration that is taking place.

The model which has been outlined will be useful in considering now certain variants of loyalist behavior.

## Loyalist Behavior as Modified by Severe Initiation and High Penalties for Exit

Loyalty has so far been hailed as a force which, in the act of postponing exit, strengthens voice and may thus save firms and organizations from the dangers of excessive or premature exit. Something has already been said, however, about situations in which loyalty does not play so providential a role. The various institutions designed to foster loyalty have obviously not been established with the purpose of elaborating an improved mixture of voice and exit; when they do so, it is unwittingly, "as a result of human action, not of human design." [8]

It is always pleasant for the social scientist to discover such hidden and unintended harmonies, but the discovery carries with it an obligation to look out for situations that fall short of harmony. In the present case, the opportunities for a nonoptimal outcome are numerous. It is possible for loyalty to overshoot the mark and thus to produce an exit-voice mix in which the exit option is unduly neglected. Secondly, it must be realized that loyalty-promoting institutions and devices are not only uninterested in stimulating voice at the expense of exit: indeed they are often meant to *repress* voice alongside exit. While feedback through exit or voice is in the long-run interest of orga-

8. This phrase, used by F. A. Hayek as the title of an essay in *Studies in Philosophy, Politics, and Economics* (Chicago: University of Chicago Press, 1967), is traced by him to Adam Ferguson's *Essay on the History of Civil Society* (1767).

nization managers, their short-run interest is to entrench themselves and to enhance their freedom to act as they wish, unmolested as far as possible by either desertions *or* complaints of members. Hence management can be relied on to think of a variety of institutional devices aiming at anything but the combination of exit and voice which may be ideal from the point of view of society.

High fees for entering an organization and stiff penalties for exit are among the main devices generating or reinforcing loyalty in such a way as to repress either exit or voice or both. How do these devices affect our model of loyalist behavior? The concept of unconscious loyalist behavior can serve to open up the subject. As was just shown, this type of behavior cannot give rise to voice; and because like all loyal behavior it also postpones exit, it will be prized by organizations whose management wishes members to refrain from both exit and voice. Such organizations will be looking for devices converting, as it were, conscious into unconscious loyalist behavior.

Actually there often is no clear dividing line between these two types of behavior, because the customer or member of the organization may have a considerable stake in *self-deception,* that is, in fighting the realization that the organization he belongs to or the product he has bought are deteriorating or defective. He will particularly tend to repress this sort of awareness if he has invested a great deal in his purchase or membership. In organizations entry into which is expensive or requires severe initiation, recognition by members of any deterioration will therefore be delayed and so will be the onset of voice. By the same token, however, it may be expected that once deterioration is adverted to, members of an organization that requires severe initiation will fight hard to prove that they were right after all in paying that high entrance fee. Thus while the onset of voice will be delayed by severe initiation, resort to it is likely to be *more active* than is ordinarily the case during a subsequent phase of loyalist

93

behavior. The high cost of entry will change the time-pattern of voice, but may well not reduce its aggregate volume.[9]

This finding implies a modification of the theory of cognitive dissonance. The theory has normally shown how people will alter their cognitions and beliefs so as to make them more consistent with some "discrepant" act or behavior they have engaged in and which is difficult to reconcile with these beliefs. In the case just noted, the act is more or less severe initiation and the cognition, in one well-known experiment, was the boring nature of the activities of the organization of which one has become a member. The theory predicted—and the experiment confirmed—that the severer the initiation the higher will be the degree of self-deception, that is, the more fascinating will the boring activities seem to the member.[10] Assume now, that there is not only some limit to self-deception but, and this is more important, room for *making* the activities of the organization more interesting as a result of members' initiative: then the same basic experimental constellation would lead to the prediction that severe-initiation members will display *more initiative* and will be *more activist* than the rest after having at first been more complacent and passive. Hence, a situation of dissonance may produce not only alterations of beliefs, attitudes, and cognitions, but could lead to *actions* designed to change the real world when that is an alternative way (and particularly when it is the only way) of overcoming or reducing dissonance.[11]

9. As is shown by the curved line in figure 1.

10. E. Aronson and J. Mills, "The Effects of Severity of Initiation on Liking for a Group," *Journal of Abnormal and Social Psychology*, 59:177–181 (1959). See also, for further refinement of the experimental results of Aronson-Mills and rebuttal of some criticisms, H. B. Gerard and G. C. Mathewson, "The Effects of Severity of Initiation on Liking for a Group: A Replication," *Journal of Experimental Social Psychology*, 2:278–287 (July 1966). See Appendix E for a fuller statement on these papers.

11. In spite of superficial resemblance, the hypothesis here proposed is fundamentally different from the one put forward and

This hypothesis is to be tested experimentally by Professor Philip Zimbardo of Stanford University and his associates.[12] Pending the outcome of these efforts, it is perhaps permissible to appeal to scattered historical evidence for illustration. Take the well-known and well-tested maxim that "revolution, like Saturn, devours its own children." Why this should be so is now easily understood: in "making the revolution" revolutionaries have paid a high personal price in risk-taking, sacrifice, and single-minded commitment. Once the revolution *is* made, a gap between the actual and the expected state of affairs is only too likely to arise. To eliminate that gap those who have paid the highest price for bringing about the new reality will be most strongly motivated to change it *anew*. In the process, they will take on some of their fellow revolutionaries who are now in positions of authority and a large number of the revolutionaries on either the one side or the other or on both will come to grief in the ensuing fight.

Another illustration of the same principle, drawn from the American experience, will be given in Chapter 8.[13]

---

tested in *When Prophecy Fails* by Leon Festinger, H. W. Riecken, and Stanley Schachter (Minneapolis: University of Minnesota Press, 1956). In this classic of the literature of cognitive dissonance, the authors investigated the effects on a group of believers of an unequivocal disconfirmation of their belief. In line with the theory's predictions, the believers became more vigorously engaged in proselyting activities than before. This activity, however, must be interpreted as an attempt to eliminate dissonance by "forgetting" the disconfirmation, *by drowning out the dissonant cognition*, rather than by changing it. Both the Aronson-Mills and the *Prophecy* situations are so constructed that the dissonant cognitions (boring nature of the activities of the group, nonoccurence of predicted flood) are unchangeable, once-and-for-all events. In the real world, many situations are of course iterative and are subject to change, "the next time around."

12. See Appendix E for a detailed statement on the scope and design of the proposed research.

13. See pp. 113–114. I argued elsewhere in a similar vein that efforts to rescue development projects from difficulty will be most vigorous when those responsible for the project are fully committed to it as a result of prior expenditures. Hence the later the difficulty appears the better, provided of course that it can be successfully solved. See Hirschman, *Development Projects Observed*, pp. 18–21.

Payment of a high price of entry thus does not lead necessarily to acquiescence with that for which the price has been paid, but may result in an even more determined and outspoken use of voice. It is also possible, of course, that by the time the member is no longer able to close his eyes to what is going on, deterioration has become such that exit appears as the only possible reaction to the sudden revelation of rottenness. Hence severe initiation may eventually activate exit as well as voice.[14] "You can actively flee and you can actively stay put"—this phrase of Erik Erikson is again most pertinent. It was quoted once before, in connection with the likely behavior of the quality-conscious consumer. The coincidence is not accidental, for severe initiation no doubt makes for quality-consciousness.

A different kind of distortion of the model of loyalist behavior occurs when an organization is able to exact a *high price for exit* (over and above the forfeit of the price for entry which occurs inevitably with exit). Such a price can range from loss of life-long associations to loss of life, with such intermediate penalties as excommunication, defamation, and deprivation of livelihood. Organizations able to exact these high penalties for exit are the most traditional human groups, such as the family, the tribe, the religious community, and the nation, as well as such more modern inventions as the gang and the totalitarian party.[15] If an organization has the ability to exact a high price for exit, it thereby acquires a powerful defense against one of the member's most potent weapons: the threat of exit. Obviously, if exit is followed by severe sanctions the very idea of exit is going to be repressed

14. The activation of exit is shown in figure 1 through the location of point *XSI* (e*X*it of members having received *S*evere *I*nitiation) ahead of *XWL*.

15. For an account of the terror of leaving the Communist party, see Gabriel A. Almond, *The Appeals of Communism* (Princeton, 1954), ch. 12.

and the threat will not be uttered for fear that the sanction will apply to the threat as well as to the act itself. In terms of the model, point $TX$ will be moved to the left and is in fact likely to disappear altogether, that is, merge with $XWL$, the point of exit when loyalty is present. This point itself may of course also be moved to the left: to deter exit is indeed a major purpose of imposing a high price for it. But in comparison with organizations that can command strong spontaneous loyalty while being unwilling or unable to impose stiff penalties for exit, the main change in members' behavior under conditions of progressive deterioration of the organization is likely to be the omission of the threat of exit rather than the postponement of exit itself.

What happens to voice in organizations where the price of exit is high? Some tentative suggestions can be advanced by distinguishing between those high-exit-price organizations where the price of entry is zero (because, as in the case of the family or nation, one enters them as a result of one's birth) and those where this price is high as well. For the latter organizations it has just been shown that the onset of felt discontent and therefore of voice will be delayed. Since the high price of exit does away, on the other hand, with the threat of exit as an effective instrument of voice, these organizations (gangs, totalitarian parties) will often be able to repress both voice and exit. In the process, they will largely deprive themselves of both recuperation mechanisms.[16]

The situation is quite different for the traditional groups, such as family and nation, which exact a high price for exit, but not for entry. Here the fact that one fully "belongs" by birthright may nurture voice and thus

16. This is a special case of the proposition, put forward by David Apter, that any increase of coercion in a society will have a price in terms of the flow of information to the powerholders. See his *Politics of Modernization* (Chicago: University of Chicago Press, 1965), p. 40.

compensate for the virtual unavailability of the threat of exit. By itself, the high price or the "unthinkability" of exit may not only fail to repress voice but may stimulate it. It is perhaps for this reason that the traditional groups which repress exit alone have proved to be far more viable than those which impose a high price for both entry and exit.

## Loyalty and the Difficult Exit from "Public Goods" (and Evils)

The reluctance to exit in spite of disagreement with the organization of which one is a member is the hallmark of loyalist behavior. When loyalty is present exit abruptly changes character: the applauded rational behavior of the alert consumer shifting to a better buy becomes disgraceful defection, desertion, and treason.

Loyalist behavior, as examined thus far, can be understood in terms of a generalized concept of penalty for exit. The penalty may be directly imposed, but in most cases it is internalized. The individual feels that leaving a certain group carries a high price with it, even though no specific sanction is imposed by the group. In both cases, the decision to remain a member and not to exit in the face of a superior alternative would thus appear to follow from a perfectly rational balancing of prospective private benefits against private costs. Loyalist behavior may, however, be motivated in a less conventional way. In deciding whether the time has come to leave an organization, members, *especially the more influential ones,* will sometimes be held back not so much by the moral and material sufferings they would themselves have to go through as a result of exit, but by the anticipation that the *organization to which they belong would go from bad to worse if they left.*

This sort of behavior is the opposite of the one discussed

in Chapter 4. It was shown there that under certain conditions the most influential members might be the first to exit. The reason for which this conclusion is reversed here is that a wholly new and somewhat strange assumption has just been introduced: the member continues to care about the activity and "output" of the organization *even after he has left it.* In most consumer-product and in many member-organization relations this is of course not the case. If I become dissatisfied with the brand of soap I usually buy, and consider switching to another, I do not expect such switching to cause a worsening of the quality of my habitual brand; even if I did I presumably would not care as long as I quit buying it.[17] With the help of this counter-example, we can spell out the two conditions that underlie the special loyalist behavior now under discussion:

In the first place, exit of a member leads to further deterioration in the quality of the organization's output; secondly, the member cares about this deterioration *whether or not he stays on as a member.*

The first condition means that quality of a product is not invariant to the number of buyers or to the amount sold. The withdrawal of some members leads to lower quality, hence presumably still lower "demand" from the remaining members and so on—a typical case of unstable equilibrium, and of a cumulative sequence à la Myrdal. The consumer-member is here a "quality-maker" rather than, as in perfect competition, a quality-taker. Situations in which individual buyers are conscious of being price-makers rather than price-takers are, of course, familiar from the theories of monopoly and monopolistic competition. What strikes the economist as weird here is the *direction* of the relationship: In the usual price-making

17. I may, in fact, entertain the opposite "serves-them-right" reaction if I hear that a firm which has disappointed me and with which I have stopped doing business comes to grief.

situation, withdrawal of a buyer (a downward shift of the demand curve) will lead to price being lowered or, correspondingly, to quality being *improved* because the supply curve is assumed to be rising. In the present case, on the contrary, withdrawal of the quality-making "buyer" leads to a quality decline. The reason is that the "buyer" is now in reality a member and as such he is involved in both the supply and the demand sides, in both production and consumption of the organization's output. Hence, if those who have the greatest influence on quality of output are also, as is likely, more quality-conscious than the rest of the members, any slight deterioration in quality may set off their exit, which in turn will lead to further deterioration, which will lead to further exits, and so on.

In this situation, utter instability is once again avoided by the intervention of loyalist behavior and particularly by members being aware of, and recoiling from, the prospective consequences of their exit. In other words, instability may be averted if members are aware that it threatens. But there is a real question why a member should care about the consequences of his exit on the quality of the organization, to the point where the prospective decline in quality would keep him from exiting. The only rational basis for such behavior is a situation in which the output or quality of the organization *matters to one even after exit*. In other words, *full exit is impossible;* in some sense, one remains a consumer of the article in spite of the decision not to buy it any longer, and a member of the organization in spite of formal exit.

This important class of situations can again be illustrated by the competition between private and public schools. Parents who plan to shift their children from public to private school may thereby contribute to a further deterioration of public education. If they realize this prospective effect of their decision they may end up by not taking it, for reasons of general welfare or even as a result of a private cost-benefit calculation : the lives of both parents and children will be affected by the quality of public education in their community, and if this quality deteriorates the higher educational attainments of the children to be obtained by shifting them to private school have a cost which could be so large as to counsel against the shift.

The distinction made by economists between private and public (or collective) goods is directly relevant to this discussion. *Public goods* are defined as goods which are consumed by all those who are members of a given community, country, or geographical area in such a manner that consumption or use by one member does not detract from consumption or use by another. Standard examples have been crime prevention and national defense as well as other accomplishments of public policies that are or ought to be enjoyed by everyone such as high international prestige or advanced standards of literacy and public health. The distinguishing characteristic of these goods is not only that they *can* be consumed by everyone, but that there is *no escape* from consuming them unless one were to leave the community by which they are provided. Thus he who says public goods says public evils. The latter result not only from universally sensed inadequacies in the supply of public goods, but from the fact that what is a public good for some—say, a plentiful supply of police dogs and atomic bombs—may well be judged a public evil by others in the same community. It is also quite easy to conceive of a public good turning into a public evil, for example, if a country's foreign and military policies develop in such a way that their "output" changes from international prestige into international disrepute. In view of this book's concern with deterioration and resulting exit or voice, this sort of possibility is of special interest.

The concept of public goods makes it easy to understand the notion that in some situations there can be no real exit from a good or an organization so that the decision to exit in the partial sense in which this may be possible must take into account any further deterioration in the good that may result. What becomes difficult to grasp, in fact, once the concept of public goods is introduced is how even a partial exit from such goods is possible.

Actually, of course, a private citizen can "get out" from public education by sending his children to private school, but at the same time he *cannot* get out, in the sense that his and his children's life will be affected by the quality of public education. There are many ostensibly private goods of this sort that one can buy or refrain from buying; but they have a "public-good dimension" (often called "externalities" by economists) so that their mere production and consumption by others affects, ennobles, or degrades the lives of all members of the community. While this is perhaps not a very frequent or very important phenomenon for saleable commodities and services, it is a central feature of many organizations in relation to their members. If I disagree with an organization, say, a political party, I can resign as a member, but generally I cannot stop being a member of the society in which the objectionable party functions. If I participate in the making of a foreign policy of which I have come to disapprove, I can resign my official policy-making position, but cannot stop being unhappy as a citizen of a country which carries on what seems to me an increasingly disastrous foreign policy. In both these examples, the individual is at first both producer and consumer of such public goods as party policy and foreign policy; he can stop being producer, but cannot stop being consumer.

It is thus possible to rationalize a wholly new type of loyalist behavior. In line with common sense (and the theory of demand), the propensity to exit has thus far been presented as a rising function of discontent with product quality, or of disagreement with the party line.

Now it can be shown that an invariant or even inverse relationship between these variables is possible. In the case of public goods, the member will compare, at any one point in the process of deterioration, the disutility, discomfort, and shame of remaining a member to the prospective damage which would be inflicted on him as a prospective nonmember and on society at large by the additional deterioration that would occur if he were to get out. The avoidance of this hypothetical damage is now the benefit of loyalist behavior, and if this benefit increases along with the cost of remaining a member, the motivation to exit need *not* become stronger as deterioration proceeds although undoubtedly our member will become increasingly unhappy. The ultimate in unhappiness and paradoxical loyalist behavior occurs when the public evil produced by the organization promises to accelerate or to reach some intolerable level as the organization deteriorates; then, in line with the reasoning just presented, the decision to exit will become ever more difficult the longer one fails to exit. The conviction that one has to stay on to prevent the worst grows stronger all the time.

Usually this sort of reasoning is an ex-post (or ex-nunc) justification of opportunism. But it must be reluctantly admitted that loyalist behavior of this type—the worse it gets the less can I afford to leave—can serve an all-important purpose when an organization is capable of dispensing public evils of truly ultimate proportions, a situation particularly characteristic of the more powerful states on the present world scene. The more wrongheaded and dangerous the course of these states the more we need *a measure of spinelessness* among the more enlightened policy makers so that some of them will still be "inside" and influential when that potentially disastrous crisis breaks out. It will be argued later that in these situations we are likely to suffer from an excess rather than from a shortage of spinelessness. It is nevertheless worth noting that the magnitude of public evils that can today be visited upon all of us by the centers of world power has bestowed "functionality" or social usefulness on protracted spine-lessness (failure to exit) provided it turns into spine (voice) at the decisive moment.

Organizations and firms producing public goods or public evils constitute the environment in which loyalist behavior (that is, postponement of exit in spite of dissatisfaction and qualms) peculiarly thrives and assumes several distinctive characteristics. For one, there is the possibility described in the last paragraphs in which we saw "right or wrong, my country" change into a seemingly perverse "the wronger the myer." Moreover, when exit does occur its nature is different from the type of exit discussed up to now. In the case of exit from organizations producing private goods, exit terminates the relationship between the customer-member and the product-organization he is leaving. True, by signaling to management that something is wrong, exit may provide a stimulus toward quality recuperation, but this effect is wholly unintended by the exiting customer-member—he "couldn't care less." In the case of public goods, on the other hand, one continues to "care" as it is impossible to get away from them entirely. In spite of exit one remains a consumer of the output or at least of its external effects from which there is no escape. Under these conditions, the customer-member will *himself* be interested in making his exit contribute to improvement of the product-organization he is leaving—an improvement which he may judge to be impossible without radical change in the way in which the organization is run. To exit will now mean to resign under protest and, in general, to denounce and fight the organization from without instead of working for change from within. In other words, the alternative is now not so much between voice and exit as between voice from within and voice from without (after exit). The exit decision then hinges on a totally new question: At what point is one more effective (besides being more at peace with oneself) fighting mistaken policies from without than continuing the attempt to change these policies from within?

The considerable difference between "proper" exit from public goods and the kind of exit (from private goods) thus far discussed is revealed when a customer-member who exits from a public good behaves *as though* he were exiting from a private one. In a society as dominated by private goods and by styles of behavior acquired in reacting to them as the United States, such confusion may perhaps be expected. Examples from recent history come easily to mind. High officials who disagree with public policies do not blast them when they resign, but present this decision as a purely private one; one leaves because a better offer has come his way, "in fairness to my family." Similarly young men and women who find American society, its values, and the actions of its government not to their tastes are "opting out" as though they could secure for themselves a better set of values and policies without having first changed the existing set. The malaise resulting from this confusion of the two kinds of exit can be measured by the relief that *would* have been experienced if at least one of the public officials "dropping out" of the Johnson administration in disagreement over Vietnam had thereupon publicly fought official war policies; and by the relief that *was* so widely felt when the 1968 campaign of Senator Eugene McCarthy made it possible for many young Americans to do just that, instead of merely "copping out."

# 8
# Exit and Voice
# in American Ideology
# and Practice

It does not take much of a plunge, at this point, to take up as our last topic a special though sizable case—that of exit and voice in relation to American ideology, tradition, and practice.

My principal point—and puzzlement—is easily stated: exit has been accorded an extraordinarily privileged position in the American tradition, but then, suddenly, it is wholly proscribed, sometimes for better, sometimes for worse, from a few key situations.

The United States owes its very existence and growth to millions of decisions favoring exit over voice. This "ultimate nature of the American experience" has been eloquently described by Louis Hartz:

> The men in the seventeenth century who fled to America from Europe were keenly aware of the oppressions of European life. But they were revolutionaries with a difference, and the fact of their fleeing is no minor fact: for it is one thing to stay at home and fight the "canon and feudal law," and it is another to leave it far behind. It is one thing to try to establish liberalism in the Old World, and it is another to establish it in the New. Revolution, to borrow the words of T. S. Eliot, means to murder and create, but the American experience has been projected strangely in the realm of creation alone. The destruction of forests and Indian tribes—heroic, bloody, legendary as it was—cannot be compared with the destruction of a social order to which one belongs oneself. The first experience is wholly external and, being external can actually be completed; the second experience is an inner struggle as well as an outer struggle, like the slaying of a Freudian father, and goes on in a sense forever.[1]

1. Louis Hartz, *The Liberal Tradition in America* (New York: Harcourt, Brace & World, 1955), pp. 64–65.

This preference for the neatness of exit over the messiness and heartbreak of voice has then "persisted throughout our national history." [2] The exit from Europe could be re-enacted within the United States by the progressive settlement of the frontier, which Frederick Jackson Turner characterized as the "gate of escape from the bondage of the past." [3] Even though the opportunity to "go West" may have been more myth than reality for large population groups in the eastern section of the country,[4] the myth itself was of the greatest importance for it provided everyone with a paradigm of problem-solving. Even after the closing of the frontier, the very vastness of the country combined with easy transportation make it far more possible for Americans than for most other people to think about solving their problems through "physical flight" than either through resignation or through ameliorating and fighting *in situ* the particular conditions into which one has been "thrown." The curious conformism of

2. Hartz, *The Liberal Tradition*, p. 65 n. Note also his phrase, in the same footnote: "In a real sense physical flight is the American substitute for the European experience of social revolution."

3. From the last paragraph of his famous 1893 paper "The Significance of the Frontier in American History," reprinted in Frederick Jackson Turner, *The Frontier in American History* (New York: Henry Holt, 1920), p. 38. Interestingly enough, Turner noted in a later essay that with the closing of the frontier new political processes, akin to "voice," would have to take the frontier's place if democracy was to be kept vigorous in the United States. "The present finds itself engaged in the task of readjusting its old ideals to new conditions and is turning increasingly to government to preserve its traditional democracy. It is not surprising that socialism shows noteworthy gains as elections continue; that parties are forming on new lines; that the demand for primary elections, for popular choice of senators, initiative, referendum, and recall, is spreading, and that the regions once the center of pioneer democracy exhibit these tendencies in the most marked degree. They are efforts to find substitutes for that former safeguard of democracy, the disappearing free lands. They are the sequence to the extinction of the frontier" (p. 321).

4. See, for example, F. A. Shannon, "A Post-Mortem on the Labor Safety-Valve Theory," *Agricultural History*, 19:31–37 (January 1945), reprinted in George R. Taylor, ed., *The Turner Thesis* (Boston: D. C. Heath & Co., 1949).

Americans, noted by observers ever since Tocqueville, may also be explained in this fashion. Why raise your voice in contradiction and get yourself into trouble as long as you can always remove yourself entirely from any given environment should it become too unpleasant?

It will be noted that all these "flights" are in the nature of true exits, that is, exits from private rather than public goods: whatever effect they had on the society that was left behind was an unintended side effect. Those who departed from their communities had no thought of improving them thereby or of fighting against them from the outside; they were immigrants rather than émigrés, and soon after their move "couldn't care less" about the fate of the communities whence they came. In this perspective, the present-day "cop-out" movement of groups like the hippies is very much in the American tradition; once again dissatisfaction with the surrounding social order leads to flight rather than fight, to withdrawal of the dissatisfied group and to its setting up a separate "scene." Perhaps, the reason for which these groups are felt to be "un-American" is not at all their act of withdrawal, but, on the contrary, their *demonstrative* "otherness" which is sensed as an attempt to influence the square society they are rejecting. By making their exit so spectacular, by oddly combining *deviance* with *defiance,* they are actually closer to voice than was the case for their pilgrim, immigrant, and pioneer forebears.

The traditional American idea of success confirms the hold which exit has had on the national imagination. Success—or, what amounts to the same thing, upward social mobility—has long been conceived in terms of evolutionary individualism.[5] The successful individual who starts out at a low rung of the social ladder, necessarily leaves his own group behind as he rises; he "passes" into, or is

5. Richard Hofstadter, *Social Darwinism in American Thought* (Philadelphia: University of Pennsylvania Press, 1945).

"accepted" by, the next higher group. He takes his immediate family along, but hardly anyone else. Success is in fact symbolized and consecrated by a succession of physical moves out of the poor quarters in which he was brought up into ever better neighborhoods. He may later finance some charitable activities designed to succor the poor or the deserving of the group and neighborhood to which he once belonged. But if an entire ethnic or religious minority group acquires a higher social status, this occurs essentially as the cumulative result of numerous, individual, uncoordinated success stories and physical moves of this kind rather than because of concerted group efforts.

The novelty of the black power movement on the American scene consists in the rejection of this traditional pattern of upward social mobility as unworkable and undesirable for the most depressed group in our society. Significantly, it combines scorn for individual penetration of a few selected blacks into white society with a strong commitment to "collective stimulation" of blacks as a group and to the improvement of the black ghetto as a place to live. In the words of one spokesman:

Integration, particularly in the token way in which it has been practiced up to now . . . elevates individual members of a group, but paradoxically, in plucking many of the most promising members from a group while failing to alter the lot of the group as a whole, weakens the collective thrust which the group might otherwise muster.[6]

This formulation is strikingly similar to the previously mentioned situations—railroads in Nigeria, public schools, and so forth—in which exit was ineffective while

6. Nathan Hare, as quoted in John H. Bunzel, "Black Studies at San Francisco State," *The Public Interest*, no. 13 (Fall 1968), p. 30. That integration, as practiced so far, deprives the black community of "leadership potential" is also argued in Stokely Carmichael and Charles V. Hamilton, *Black Power* (New York: Vintage Books, 1967), p. 53.

voice was fatally weakened by exit of the most quality-conscious customers of a firm or of the most valuable members of an organization.

In the case of a minority that has been discriminated against a further argument can often be made: namely, that exit is bound to be unsatisfactory and unsuccessful even from the point of view of the individuals who practice it. The point is familiar, but it may be of interest to see it made not for "passing" Jews or Negroes in the United States, but for Andean Indians:

A normal pattern of change in the Andes is for the individual to become a mestizo by leaving his highland community of birth, rejecting his Indian background, and assuming all possible mestizo status symbols. The individual who becomes a mestizo by this route, however, finds himself part of a despised "cholo" minority in a world dominated by urban upper classes to which he cannot aspire.[7]

This unsatisfactory process of individual mobility is then compared to the group process which, according to the author, was made possible in Bolivia by the Revolution:

In the formerly Indian communities of Bolivia, on the other hand, the group itself is the agency regulating the adoption of the mestizo traits. The individuals within the group proceed at the same pace, with few persons standing out as "more mestizo" than the others. Neither is there strong motivation physically to leave the community nor to reject identifiably Indian behavior patterns. Rather, the individuals are participating in a true cultural change, as a group . . . There is no rush to acquire status symbols, because there is a deep sense of the ridiculousness of a person wearing a necktie, for example, when that person is unable to speak Spanish.[8]

7. Richard Patch, "Bolivia: The Restrained Revolution," *The Annual of the American Academy of Political and Social Sciences*, 334:130 (1961).
8. *Ibid.*

A similar preference for the "collective thrust" approach over the "flight" or "melting pot" pattern of upward social mobility has been characteristic of spokesmen for seriously lagging regions within countries, such as Italy's South and Brazil's Northeast. In plans to catch up with the rest of the country, these spokesmen have usually assigned a quite minor role to emigration which they tended to consider not as a contribution to their region's uplift, but as an unfortunate "hemorrhage" of its best talent.

That upward social mobility of just the talented few from the lower classes can make domination of the lower by the upper classes even more secure than would be achieved by rigid separation, becomes evident if one imagines a society that would have a systematic policy of *adopting* promising low-class youngsters into upper-class families. Adoption practices of this sort can be found in Japan during the Tokugawa period when that country indeed enjoyed "two centuries of peace and stability." [9]

In practice upward mobility for a disadvantaged or hitherto oppressed group is likely to require a mixture of the individual and the group process, that is, a mixture of exit and voice. The group process will come into prominence at certain intermediate stages, and there is special need for it when social cleavages have been protracted and when economic disparities are reinforced by religious, ethnic, or color barriers. In the United States, in fact, reality has often been different from ideology: as is well recognized, ethnic minorities have risen in influence and

9. R. P. Dore, "Talent and the Social Order in Tokugawa Japan," in John W. Hall and Marius E. Jansen, eds., *Studies in the Institutional History of Early Modern Japan* (Princeton: Princeton University Press, 1968), pp. 349, 354. The imagination of Michael Young takes the process one step further. In his anti-utopia where the upper and lower classes are increasingly separated as a result of individual mobility there develops a "disturbing growth in the black market of baby traffic, stupid babies from elite homes being sent, sometimes with princely dowries, in exchange for clever ones from the lower classes." *The Rise of Meritocracy* (1958, Penguin Books, 1968 edition), p. 184.

status not only through the cumulative effect of individual success stories, but also because they formed interest groups, turned into outright majorities in some political subdivisions, and became pivotal in national politics.* Nevertheless, the black power doctrine represents a totally new approach to upward mobility because of its open advocacy of the group process. It had immense shock value because it spurned and castigated a supreme value of American society—success via exit from one's group.

Apart from such latter-day dissonant voices, the ideology of exit has been powerful in America. With the country having been founded on exit and having thrived on it, the belief in exit as a fundamental and beneficial social mechanism has been unquestioning. It may account for the strength of the national faith in the virtues of such institutions as the two-party system and competitive enterprise; and, in the latter case, for the national *disbelief* in the economist's notion that a market dominated by two or three giant firms departs substantially from the ideal competitive model. As long as one can transfer his allegiance from the product of firm $A$ to the competing product of firm $B$, the basic symbolism of the national love affair with exit is satisfied.

Yet, as love may suddenly turn into hate, so can the national infatuation with exit give way in certain crucial areas to its utter proscription. To some extent, exit is itself responsible for the emergence of its opposite. In leaving his country the emigrant makes a difficult decision and usually pays a high price in severing many strong affective ties. Additional payment is extracted as he is being initiated into a new environment and adjusting to it. The result is a strong psychological compulsion to like that for

* For some forceful and well documented remarks along these lines, see Christopher Lasch, *The Agony of the American Left* (New York: Alfred A. Knopf, 1969), pp. 134–141.

which so large a payment has been made. In retrospect, the "old country" will appear more abominable than ever while the new country will be declared to be the greatest, "the last best hope of mankind," and all manner of other superlatives. And one must be happy. Probably because of this collective compulsion to be happy, the word has gradually taken on a much weaker meaning than it has in other languages. This is illustrated in the story about two immigrants from Germany meeting for the first time after many years in New York. One asks the other: "Are you happy here?" Reply: "I am happy, *aber glücklich bin ich nicht*." [10]

As a country's central bank is the lender of last resort, so has the United States long been the "country of last resort." To most of its citizens—with the important exception of those whose forefathers came as slaves—exit from the country has long been peculiarly unthinkable.

Suppose, however, things are not fully satisfactory— what then? In line with the earlier argument about the effects of a high price of entry on loyalty, it may be expected that the point at which one avows any qualms will be postponed. This is precisely the phase of compulsive happiness. Situations may well arise, however, in which qualms can no longer be repressed. A number of reactions are then possible:

(1) As was just shown, another exit may be attempted, but this time within the (fortunately wide) confines of the country.

10. Translation: "but happy I am not." As another example of the intensity associated with the word "happy" in non-American languages, take the opening lines of a poem by Umberto Saba:

In quel momento ch'ero giá felice
(Dio mi perdoni la parola grande
e tremenda) . . .

which translates feebly into: "At that time when I was still happy (may God forgive me the great and awesome word) . . ." Saba, *Il Canzoniere* (Rome: Giulio Einaudi, 1945), p. 220.

(2) Since clearly the country cannot be at fault, responsibility for unhappiness, qualms, and so forth is assumed to lie with the person experiencing these sensations. Another dose of "adjustment" is in order.

(3) Finally, if the country is too obviously at fault after all, it has to be *made* into that ideal place which one wants it so passionately to be. Hence voice will come into its own with unusual force. It will be animated by the typically American conviction that human institutions can be perfected and that problems can be solved. The compulsion to be happy is replaced by the compulsion to use voice for the purpose of making the country live up to its image. It is, in fact, to this compulsion that the country owes some of its greatest achievements just as it owes its origin to exit.

If the rejection of the exit option in the American setting were limited to exit from the country, there would be little cause for worry. The phenomenon has, however, taken lately a different and far less benign form: the extreme reluctance of Americans in public office to resign in protest against policies with which they disagree.

The preceding considerations are relevant here. Many of the reasons for which the United States citizen finds it impossible to consider exit from his country apply, in only slightly altered form, to the high official as he considers exit from the government. As the former cannot bring himself to contemplate exit from the "best" country, so the latter has an overwhelming desire not to sever his ties with the "best" country's government which, moreover, is the world's most powerful. This inability to resign applies to men on opposite sides of the political spectrum who were known to disagree strongly with official policies, to a General MacArthur as well as to an Adlai Stevenson. In 1966, the latter's predicament was satirized in *MacBird!* where the "Egg of Head" weighs exit and voice and finds exit wanting in attractiveness:

In speaking out one loses influence.
The chance for change by pleas and prayer is gone.
The chance to modify the devil's deeds
As critic from within is still my hope.
To quit the club! Be outside looking in!
This outsideness, this unfamiliar land,
From which few travellers ever get back in . . .
I fear to break; I'll work within for change.[11]

Two agonizing war years later, the continued reluctance of high officials with "qualms" to break with the Johnson administration was searchingly analyzed, together with a number of other bureaucratic aspects of the conflict, in an article written by a former insider, James C. Thomson, Jr.[12] One of his principal points of explanation was what he calls the *domestication of dissenters,* which is achieved through "assigning" the role of "official dissenter" or devil's advocate to the doubters within the government. In the process, the doubter's conscience is assuaged, but at the same time his position is made explicit *and predictable.* This predictability means a fatal loss of power for him; his position becomes discountable.[13] The dissenter is allowed to recite his piece on condition that he engages in

11. Barbara Garson, *MacBird!* (New York: Grassy Knoll Press, 1966), pp. 22–23.

12. James C. Thomson, Jr., "How could Vietnam Happen? An Autopsy," *Atlantic Monthly* (April 1968), pp. 47–53.

13. As Thomson put it: "Once Mr. Ball began to express doubts, he was warmly institutionalized: he was encouraged to become the inhouse devil's advocate on Vietnam. The upshot was inevitable: the process of escalation allowed for periodic requests to Mr. Ball to speak his piece; Ball felt good, I assume (he had fought for righteousness); the others felt good (they had given a full hearing to the dovish option); and there was minimal unpleasantness. The club remained intact; and it is of course possible that matters would have gotten worse faster if Mr. Ball had kept silent, or left before his final departure in the fall of 1966. There was also, of course, the case of the last institutionalized doubter, Bill Moyers. The President is said to have greeted his arrival at meetings with an affectionate, 'Well, here comes Mr. Stop-the-Bombing'" (p. 49). That power in a bureaucratic situation varies inversely with predictability is pointed out convincingly by Michel Crozier, *The Bureaucratic Phenomenon* (Chicago: University of Chicago Press, 1964), ch. 6.

"role-playing" as "a member of the team." In this way, he is made to give up in advance his strongest weapon: the threat to resign under protest.

Obviously, the bargain is a very poor one for the dissenter, so the question arises: Why would he stand for it? In attempting an answer, several of the points made in the preceding chapter can be invoked. First of all, in view of the potential of frightfulness at the government's command, the final policy decision can always be made to look as some middle course between the two opposing points of view of "hawks" and "doves"; hence members of both dissenting groups are always made to feel that "if it had not been for me, an even more sinister decision would have been taken." The dove in particular will argue that it is his duty to remain at his post, however much he may "suffer." Considering the enormous power for good and particularly for evil that he sees constantly being displayed around him, even the tiniest influence seems to him worth exerting. His reasoning actually contains a kernel of truth as was shown in the discussion of exit from public goods. But this is precisely the source of the trouble. Opportunism can in this situation be rationalized as public-spirited; even better, it can masquerade as secret martyrdom. Given so delicious a mixture of motives, opportunistic behavior will be indulged in with an intensity, persistence and abandon out of all proportion with its justification. The dove will vastly overestimate his influence as well as the damaging consequences of his exit upon the course of events. It would seem that Lord Acton's famous dictum can be varied to read: "Power corrupts; and even a little influence in a country with huge power corrupts hugely."

The prospect that exit will be badly neglected in this situation can be made plausible in a different way. It was argued in Chapter 4 that deterioration in the lower-quality ranges of a commodity is likely to lead to exit much more promptly than in the upper- or top-quality ranges. In case of deterioration of low- or medium-quality merchandise, exit comes easily to a customer since a nondeteriorated variety of similar price or quality range is always available as a substitute. The customer of the upper- or top-quality varieties is likely to be much less amply served with ready alternatives, should his variety begin to disappoint him; hence he will be more inclined to use voice, to "work from within." Can one infer that it is easier to exit from the (deteriorating) government of a minor or medium-sized nation than from that of a major world power? Obviously not in any strict sense, for it is impossible to invoke the market mechanism in the latter situation: if one's own government deteriorates one does not usually "go over" to another. An analogous mechanism may, nevertheless, be at work. A small or medium-sized country has many "colleagues" and its behavior can be compared to that of others in the same class. Standards of behavior for the government of such a country are recognizable. It is possible to tell when they are flouted. No similar standard of comparison is available for the superpower which can claim, with some plausibility, that in view of its special burdens and responsibilities ordinary standards do not apply to its actions. This may be another reason for which the decision to exit from the government of the most powerful country is particularly and deplorably infrequent.

Why "deplorably"? Because exit has an essential role to play in restoring quality performance of government, just as in any organization. It will operate either by making the government reform or by bringing it down, but in any event, the jolt provoked by clamorous exit of a respected member is in many situations an indispensable complement to voice. A case in point was Senator Eugene McCarthy's decision to run for President, a decision which had a powerful influence on events. This was an exit from the club of top Democratic politicians, a breaking of the rules of the game as traditionally played within the governing party (the rule being that one does not oppose the President's bid for reelection). But there was to occur no similarly clamorous exit from the President's "official family" in spite of the increasing misgivings of several members of that family. Having been first satirized and analyzed by Barbara Garson and James Thomson, respectively, this reluctance to exit has been increasingly recognized as a national problem and even scandal. Thus James Reston wrote in a postmortem on the Johnson administration:

One thing that is fairly clear from the record is that the art of resigning on principle from positions close to the top of the American Government has almost disappeared. Nobody quits now, as Anthony Eden and Duff Cooper left Neville Chamberlain's Cabinet, with a clear and detailed explanation of why they couldn't be identified with the policy any longer . . . Most [of those who stayed on] at the critical period of escalation gave to the President the loyalty they owed to the country. Some . . . are now wondering in private life whether this was in the national interest.[14]

14. *The New York Times* (March 9, 1969). Note also the much earlier complaint by John Osborne: "We should know by now, I suppose, that officials in our day do not quit for a cause . . . But I must say, with due respect for George Ball . . . that an occasional resignation for the sake of principle would improve the Washington scene and deter, or maybe even prevent, errors of conception and judgment of the kind that he cites and bemoans." *The New Republic* (June 15, 1968), p. 27. As the proofs of this book are being corrected, it is fortunately possible to record a first break in this pattern: in October 1969, six analysts of the RAND Corporation sent a carefully reasoned letter to the *New York Times* and the *Washington Post* advocating unilateral, speedy, and total withdrawal of United States forces from Vietnam. In the nature of the case, such direct communication with the press comes very close to resignation under protest. It is public protest against official policies which RAND services through its contracts with the Defense Department. While the protesters do not exit, they evidently assume the risk of "being exited." (*Washington Post*, October 12, 1969.) As this book goes into a new printing (September 1971), a further addition is of interest: The letter, with its original mixture of exit and voice, was largely due to Daniel Ellsberg, one of the six signers.

But the moral condemnation or exhortation implicit in this kind of writing is not likely to be very effective, given the very strong reasons for eschewing exit which have been noted. It is more helpful to cast around for institutional devices designed to activate exit under protest, just as we have earlier searched for ways of facilitating voice. Along such lines Thomson has argued that resignation under protest is particularly unattractive for the American Cabinet member because, unlike his British counterpart, he has no "parliamentary backbench to which to retreat." [15] In general he has ordinarily no base in politics or in public opinion. Recent suggestions that members of the Cabinet and perhaps other high officials should be drawn from interest group leaders or should otherwise have some group following, deserve close study in this connection. Such persons would presumably be less easily caught in what might be called the *member-of-the-team trap*.

15. Thomson, "How Could Vietnam Happen?"

# 9

# The Elusive Optimal Mix of Exit and Voice

In the earlier chapters of this volume, much has been made of situations in which exit drives out voice and assumes a disproportionate share of the burden involved in guiding a firm or organization back to efficiency after the initial lapse. It was shown that, in certain situations, voice could function as a valuable mechanism of recuperation and deserves to be strengthened by appropriate institutions. With a commendable sense of balance I have turned my attention, in the last few pages, to situations in which it is the exit option's turn to be almost wholly shunned, much to the detriment, once again, of effective recovery. Having come full circle I shall stop very soon. But in view of the numerous baroque ornamentations which have been added to the circle as it was being traced a somewhat schematic finale may be useful.

First it is worth recapitulating how organizations array themselves in a table whose classification criterion is the absence or presence of our two reaction mechanisms. It hardly needs saying that this table is by way of a very rough summary. Qualifications to the pigeonholing here presented and borderline cases have been noted throughout the book.

This table brings out the basic contrast between organizations receiving information on member-customer discontent essentially through exit and hardly at all through voice such as business firms in a competitive market, and the more traditional human groupings exit from which is virtually unheard of while voice is available to the members in varying degrees. Organizations where both exit and voice play important roles are relatively few : the most important ones are voluntary associations of various types

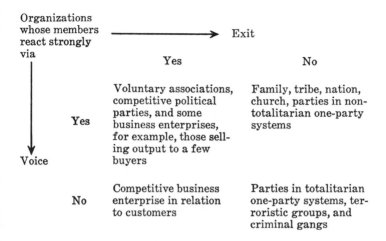

| Organizations whose members react strongly via | | Exit | |
|---|---|---|---|
| | | Yes | No |
| Voice | Yes | Voluntary associations, competitive political parties, and some business enterprises, for example, those selling output to a few buyers | Family, tribe, nation, church, parties in non-totalitarian one-party systems |
| | No | Competitive business enterprise in relation to customers | Parties in totalitarian one-party systems, terroristic groups, and criminal gangs |

including, as a most important subcategory, competitive political parties. Also, certain types of clients of business firms will often attempt to influence the firms' policies directly instead of choosing exit.

There are probably no organizations that are wholly immune to either exit or voice on the part of their members. The ones that have been listed in the cell corresponding to that category are those that, in their intended structure, make no explicit or implicit allowance for either mechanism. Exit is here considered as treason and voice as mutiny. Such organizations are likely to be less viable, in the long run, than the others; exit and voice being illegal and severely penalized, they will be engaged in only when deterioration has reached so advanced a stage that recovery is no longer either possible or desirable. Moreover, at this stage, voice and exit will be undertaken with such strength that their effect will be destructive rather than reformist.

On the other hand, there is no implication in the table that the organizations which are equipped with both feedback mechanisms are necessarily more advanced or viable than those which rely primarily on one alone. All depends on the responsiveness of the organization to whatever mechanism or combination of mechanisms it is equipped with. If an organization equipped with exit is extremely sensitive to the loss of customers or members all is for the best; and similarly for an organization equipped with voice that takes complaints and protests from its members very seriously. But what if an organization is not particularly sensitive to the particular reaction it happens to provoke or does not possess the mechanism to which it would be sensitive? A large part of this book has been devoted to such cases of inadequate or wrong responses and the argument can be summarized by means of another table.

|  | Decline arouses primarily: | |
|---|---|---|
|  | Exit | Voice |
| Exit | Competitive business enterprise (for qualifications see Chapter 2) | Organizations where dissent is allowed, but is "institutionalized" |
| Organization is sensitive primarily to: |  |  |
| Voice | Public enterprise subject to competition from an alternative mode, lazy oligopolist, corporation-shareholder relations, inner cities, etc. | Democratically responsive organizations commanding considerable loyalty from members |

The greatest interest centers here naturally on those "perverse" or pathological cases where an organization is in effect equipped with a reaction mechanism to which it is not responsive: those who are affected by quality decline do vent their feelings in one way or another, but management happens to be inured or indifferent to their particular reaction and thus does not feel compelled to correct its course. The situations of this type which have been described at greatest length, particularly in Chapters 4 and 5, involved organizations whose decline gives rise to exit that does not bother management nearly as much as might be the case for voice. In Chapter 8, however, a situation of the symmetrically opposite type was encountered: an organization—the Executive Branch of the United States government—whose deteriorating performance under Lyndon Johnson led to numerous, but futile manifestations of voice when exit might have been more effective.

Several conclusions follow from the general observation that an organization may be arousing, through its decline, one kind of reaction from its members when its recovery would be more powerfully stimulated by another kind. One advantage of this formulation is that it points immediately to a *variety* of remedies or a *combination* of them. Take the case where an organization arouses primarily exit to which it is far more insensitive than it would be to voice. Corrective policies obviously include efforts to make the organization more responsive to exit, *but also* efforts to have the members of the organization switch from exit to voice. In this fashion, the range of possible remedial measures is broadened. For example, when railroads do not react vigorously to the loss of customers the typical proposal is to introduce stronger "financial disciplines" in the hope that the railroad managers will then react to the loss of revenue like private enterprise threatened by bankruptcy. It is now clear that as an alternative or complementary step it is worth looking into ways and means of strengthening voice on the part of the customers. This can be done directly, by reducing the cost and increasing the rewards of voice, as well as indirectly, by raising the cost of exit and even by reducing the opportunities for it.

Similarly, when an organization arouses but ignores voice while it would be responsive to exit, thought must be given both to making exit more easy and attractive by appropriately redesigned institutions and to making the organization more responsive to voice. The approach to the improvement of institutional designs that is advocated here widens the spectrum of policy choices that are usually considered and it avoids the strong opposite biases in favor of either exit or voice which come almost naturally to the economist and political scientist, respectively.[1]

But a word of caution is now needed about what our approach *cannot* yield: it does not come out with a firm prescription for some optimal mix of exit or voice, nor does it wish to accredit the notion that each institution requires its own mix that could be gradually approached by trial and error. At any one point of time, it is possible to say that there is a deficiency of one or the other of our two mechanisms; but it is very unlikely that one could specify a most efficient mix of the two that would be stable over time. The reason is simple: *each recovery mechanism is itself subject to the forces of decay which have been invoked here all along.* This is so not just to add a final touch of philosophical consistency, but for more mundane reasons as well. As has already been mentioned, the short-run interest of management in organizations is to increase its own freedom of movement; management will therefore strain to strip the members-customers of the weapons which they can wield, be they exit or voice, and to convert, as it were, what should be a feedback into a safety valve. Thus voice can become mere "blowing off steam" as it is being emasculated by the institutionalization and domestication of dissent which was described toward the end of the previous chapter. And exit can be similarly blunted. As was shown, organizations and firms that are ostensibly competing and are normally sensitive to exit can learn to play a cooperative, collusive game in the course of which they take in each other's disgruntled customers or members. To the extent that the game is played successfully by competing organizations or firms, exit, compensated as it is by entry, ceases to be a serious threat to the deteriorating organizations.

1. See the discussion of the Friedman proposal on education in ch. 1, above.

While management thus finds ways of whittling down the effectiveness of the reaction mode that, in any given set of circumstances, appears to be preferred by consumer-members, the latter are in a way easing management's task by relying evermore on this mode and letting the other atrophy. As was mentioned at various times (particularly with regard to voice), the effectiveness of the less familiar mode becomes not only more uncertain, but tends to be *increasingly underestimated*. The reason is that effective use of the less familiar mechanism requires that its power be discovered or rediscovered whereas the preferred mechanism is routinely familiar; since quite properly we dare not believe in creative discoveries until they have happened, we will underestimate the effectiveness of *voice* when *exit* is dominant and vice versa. Once members have a slight preference for, say, voice over exit, a cumulative movement sets in which makes exit look ever less attractive and more inconceivable. As a result, voice will be increasingly relied on by members at a time when management is working hard to make itself less vulnerable to it.

For these reasons, conditions are seldom favorable for the emergence of any stable and optimally effective mix of exit and voice. Tendencies toward exclusive reliance on one mode and toward a decline in its effectiveness are likely to develop and only when the dominant mode plainly reveals its inadequacy will the other mode eventually be injected once again.

The invigorating results that can be achieved by the shock effect of such an injection have recently been demonstrated when the consumers' *voice* was suddenly introduced, primarily through the courage and enterprise of Ralph Nader, into an area where exit had long been the dominant and almost exclusive mode. In the opposite case, when voice is the dominant reaction mode, exit can be similarly galvanizing. It may be asked why this should be so, why exit, an act of withdrawal, should suddenly prove

125

to be influential when the returns from "working from within" via voice have been declining. Exit is not usually undertaken for the purpose of gaining more influence than one had as a member. That is nevertheless the way it often works out, especially when exit is a highly unusual event. Social psychologists have noticed that "the disappearance of the source of communication leads to a change of opinion in its favor." [2] Exit is unsettling to those who stay behind as there can be no "talking back" to those who have exited. By exiting one renders his arguments unanswerable. The remarkable influence wielded by martyrs throughout history can be understood in those terms, for the martyr's death is exit at its most irreversible and argument at its most irrefutable.

The critique of the optimal mix concept thus leads to a triple suggestion. In order to retain their ability to fight deterioration those organizations that rely primarily on one of the two reaction mechanisms need an occasional injection of the other. Other organizations may have to go through regular cycles in which exit and voice alternate as principal actors. Finally, an awareness of the inborn tendencies toward instability of any optimal mix may be helpful in improving the design of institutions that need both exit and voice to be maintained in good health.

It is even conceivable that this book might have a more direct influence. By bringing out the hidden potential of whatever reaction mode is currently neglected, it could encourage resort to either exit or voice, as the case may be. Such at least is the stuff writers' dreams are made of.

2. Serge Moscovici, "Active Minorities, Social Influence and Social Change," a paper prepared at the Center for Advanced Study in the Behavioral Sciences, 1968–1969, p. 31. In support of this point, Moscovici quotes experimental results of Muzafer Sherif and Carl I. Hovland.

Appendixes
Index

# Appendix A.
## A Simple Diagrammatic Representation
## of Voice and Exit *

A slight modification of the traditional demand diagram makes it possible to show the manner in which exit and voice are generated as a result of quality deterioration. In the following, the quality-elasticity of demand, that is, the exit-response of consumers to downward changes in quality, is assumed to be given, without regard to the possibility and prospective effectiveness of voice.

Figure 2a shows demand as a function of quality, measured along the vertical axis, rather than of price. Distance from the origin increases the poorer the quality; in this fashion the demand curve retains its usual downward slope. Normal quality is shown by point $L_0$, while post-lapse quality is shown by $L_1$. Figure 2b gives the conventional representation of unit price along the vertical axis. Both figures show quantity bought on the horizontal axis. When quality drops from $L_0$ to $L_1$ with unit price remaining unchanged, demand declines from $Q_0$ to $Q_1$ and total revenue losses are shown on figure 2b by the area of the rectangle $Q_1Q_0P'_0T$. This is the exit or "$E$" rectangle. To what extent this revenue loss will curtail or perhaps wipe out the firm's profits depends of course on cost conditions which are not shown here.

Voice, on the other hand, depends on the number of non-exiting customers $OQ_1$ and on the degree of deterioration $L_0L_1$ in figure 2a. Hence the amount of voice likely to be forthcoming is proportional to the area of the rectangle $L_0TP_1L_1$. This is the voice or "$V$" rectangle.

In general the $E$ and $V$ rectangles are not directly additive. But for any drop in quality, exit and voice somehow combine to exert influence on management; if the share of each in the total influence could be estimated, one could draw, for this drop, the vertical scale of the price diagram (figure 2b) so that the $E$ and $V$ rectangles would represent correctly their respective influence shares. Figure 2, for example, has been drawn so as to show that when quality declines from $L_0$ to $L_1$, exit will be twice as

* See text pages 22–23 and 33–36.

Appendix A

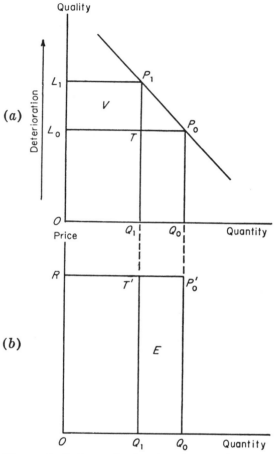

Figure 2. Voice and exit when demand is a function of quality

effective as voice. If, within a certain range, the effectiveness of both voice and exit depend exclusively on, and vary directly with, their rectangle areas, then the decisive factor in determining the shares of voice and exit in the aggregate amount of pressure that is brought to bear on the firm is the quality-elasticity of demand. Under these conditions, higher elasticity means higher aggregate effectiveness of voice and exit only if it is assumed that the negative effect on recuperation due to the decline in the voice rectangle is more than compensated by the increase in the exit rectangle.

Voice can inflict direct costs on management as complaining customers occupy the time of the firm's personnel and succeed in having defective merchandise "fixed up" or exchanged. To the extent that this is the case, voice has directly adverse monetary consequences which could then be represented in figure 2b. Suppose, for example, that half of the nonexiting customers complain and that the average complaint results in a cost that amounts to one-half of the article's sales price; then voice would inflict a monetary loss equal to one-fourth of the $ORT'Q_1$ rectangle. (Note that voice acts directly on profits while exit acts on profits via revenue.) It should be emphasized, however, that the effectiveness of voice does not at all *depend* on being convertible in this fashion into the measuring rod of money. Some comments closely related to this point appear on pages 72–74.

# Appendix B.
## The Choice Between
## Voice and Exit *

This note attempts to explore in a more formal way the alternative between exit and voice from the point of view of the individual customer of a product whose quality has declined. In figure 3 quality is shown on the horizontal axis (this time it im-

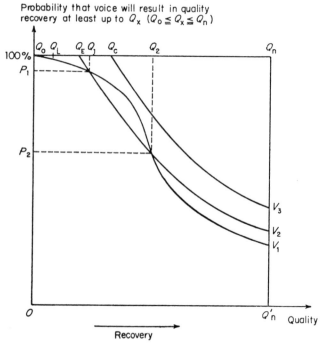

Figure 3. The choice between voice and exit as a function of members' influence and attitude toward risk

proves as it moves away from the origin) while the vertical axis now measures the cumulative probability, as appraised by the customer, that *at least* a given quality improvement will be achieved by voice. The original "normal" quality is shown as $Q_n$

* See text pages 36–40.

and it is assumed that quality has deteriorated to the point $Q_o$. Any point in the rectangle $OQ_oQ_nQ'_n$ represents a quality improvement associated to the probability, as estimated by the member or customer, that at least such an improvement will actually be achieved. Customers are likely to be indifferent between a small improvement in relation to $Q_o$ associated with a high probability that at least this improvement will be obtained (within some reasonable time period) and the inverse combination of the two variables. Two indifference curves of this type are shown; they are likely to be convex toward the origin for the reason that the customer will be increasingly reluctant to accept lower probabilities of recovery for the sake of improved quality. Points $V_1$, $V_2$, and $V_3$ represent completely successful outcomes of the voice option: in all these cases, quality is fully restored to its "normal" level, but the probability of this result varies.

The exit option can be represented by a point such as $Q_E$, indicating through its position between $Q_o$ and $Q_n$ that the closest competing or substitute product is superior in quality to $Q_o$ but inferior to $Q_n$—the latter relationship must hold if the competing product was not chosen when quality of the now deteriorated product stood at $Q_n$. In the most straightforward interpretation of the diagram, prices of the two competing products are assumed to be the same, but it will be shown later that point $Q_E$ can also be understood to represent a competing product which differs from the deteriorating one with respect to both quality and price.[1] The coordinate of $Q_E$ indicates that, in contrast to voice, there is no uncertainty whatever about what exit would bring—the competing product exists as a beckoning alternative and is there for all to see. The indifference curve going through $Q_E$ (shown as curve $Q_EV_2$) is the locus of all those combinations of quality improvements and chances to achieve them (or better) that would make it hard for the consumer to make up his mind between exit and waiting for the results of voice. But all points northeast of $Q_EV_2$ (in $OQ_oQ_nQ'_n$) would show combinations of quality improvement and probabilities of success of voice where the contest between voice and exit would be won by the former while the area southwest of $Q_EV_2$

1. See below, Appendix D, n. 4.

shows combinations that are inferior to $E$ and would therefore lead to exit.

The choice between exit and voice turns out to be a real-life situation in which people are confronted with the choice postulated by modern (von Neumann-Morgenstern) utility theory for the purpose of constructing utility functions: the customer-member chooses between two alternative courses of action, one of which (exit) brings a given result with complete certainty whereas the other (voice) constitutes a lottery option or probability mixture leading, once again, to two outcomes. As in the theoretical construct, one of these outcomes is superior to the certain result of the exit option while the other is inferior to it (or is not unequivocally superior to it). The specific probability contemplated by the person considering the voice option is the probability $(p)$ that voice will achieve at least a given improvement of quality over $Q_o$. The decision maker who stands at $Q_o$ faces the choice between $Q_E$ and the probability mixture $[p, \overset{\geqq}{Q_x}; (1 - p), \overset{<}{Q_x}]$ where $\overset{\geqq}{Q_x}$ stands for any quality equal to or higher than $Q_x$ (up to $Q_n$) and $\overset{<}{Q_x}$ for any quality from $Q_o$ up to but not including $Q_x$. The indifference curves result from compensating variations of the $p$'s and the $Q_x$'s. With $p$ equal to unity, that is, if the result of voice were known with certainty, the customer would choose exit whenever $Q_x < Q_E$, and voice whenever $Q_x > Q_E$ and he would be indifferent between the two options (provided voice is costless and its result instantaneous) if $Q_x = Q_E$. Thus, in the case of certainty, the choice depends only on the position of $Q_E$ with respect to $Q_o$ and $Q_n$, that is, on the degree of substitutability of the competing commodity for the deteriorating one. But if the outcome of voice is uncertain, the willingness to bear the risk of voice obviously is an additional important factor in the customer's decision.

In addition to knowing his own preferences, the customer or member contemplating the voice option may be assumed to have some idea of the probabilities attaching to the actual achievement of various degrees of success (success being measured by the extent to which recovery of normal quality is achieved). The resulting probability distribution results in an "influence curve" such as $Q_o V_1$ which shows for every improvement of quality over $Q_0$ the probability that at least this improvement will actually be attained as a result of voice. The influence curve is a cumulative probability distribution. If the corresponding point distribution were of normal shape, the cumulative distribution would have the symmetrical $S$-shape shown. The curve starts at $Q_0$ as the chances that the result of voice will be nil or better are obviously 100 percent, drops steeply in the vicinity of the most likely result of voice, and intercepts the $Q_n Q'_n$ line because of the optimistic assumption that the chances of total recovery resulting from voice are better than zero.

Is it possible to read off from the positions of the influence curve and of the indifference curve going through $Q_E$ whether a consumer will choose exit or voice? Unfortunately this is none too easy. All one can say is that election of the voice option is the more probable the greater the area of overlap between the two curves. Voice will win out if the actual improvement due to voice exceeds the improvements that are minimally required in view of the availability of exit over a wide range of desired quality improvements. Similarly, the voice option will be chosen if the likely chances of success of voice exceed the maximally acceptable risk (again in view of the availability of the exit option) for a wide range of chances on which the consumer may focus. In the case shown the consumer will choose voice if he focuses on any point between $Q_1$ and $Q_2$ as the desired quality or on any point between $P_1$ and $P_2$ as an acceptable risk. But he will choose exit if he happens to focus either on full recovery or on very low-risk outcomes of voice such as those that can be obtained with a degree of probability higher than $P_1$.[2]

Effective ways of bringing voice to bear are frequently only discovered in the course of members' attempts to use it, as is stressed at various points in the text. To the extent that this is so, the effectiveness of voice will be *underestimated* at the moment at which the choice between exit and voice has to be made. One possible offset to this underestimate is to sense exit

2. If the customer or member who must decide between exit and voice takes into account only the expected value of the probability distribution, then he has only one point of this distribution to worry about and the position of this point in relation to the indifference curve going through $Q_E$ will yield a clearcut decision.

as costly because of loyalty to the deteriorating product or organization (see Chapter 7). In terms of the present diagram, costliness of exit because of loyalty could be registered by a movement of point $Q_E$ to the left and up to, say, $Q_L$ indicating that the quality of the competing product becomes attractive not when it is intrinsically superior but when its margin of superiority is sufficient to cancel out the "cost of disloyalty" that is incurred when the member-customer goes over to it. It is of course conceivable that point $Q_L$ lies to the left of $Q_o$; in this case the exit option would be ruled out entirely.

Correspondingly the diagram can take account of the possible direct cost of voice. If voice requires an expenditure of time and money, then resort to it will not take place unless it produces a quality improvement *over and above* that available through exit. If $Q_E Q_C$ is this extra quality improvement needed for voice to be worthwhile, then the indifference curve starting at $Q_C$, rather than that starting with $Q_E$, is the borderline between the two realms of exit and voice.

It would be possible to complicate the analysis further by showing a family of influence curves corresponding to different volumes or intensities of voice that might be forthcoming. In that case, different costs would have to be attached to these different volumes and one might then define theoretically an optimal volume of voice that would maximize "return" over "cost." The unique influence curve shown in the diagram can be viewed as this optimal curve. An alternative interpretation is available in a situation in which each individual's voice is only a very small component of the aggregate amount of voice that is likely to be forthcoming. In that case, the individual will make a double estimate: first he estimates the total volume of voice (including his own) that is likely to be forthcoming and then he estimates the likely achievements of this "objective" volume of voice.

It should be obvious that figure 3 represents the choice situation facing an individual customer or member. When exit and voice are viewed as alternative courses of action in this way, some customers will choose exit and others voice because they have different preference maps, entertain different estimates of their influence and of the cost of using that influence, and even make different evaluations of the extent to which the competing product is an acceptable substitute for the deteriorating one. In the terms of the diagram, not only the shape of the indifference and influence curves and the location of point $C$ are likely to differ from one customer to another, but also the position of point $E$, as is shown in Appendix D, footnote 4.

# Appendix C.
## The Reversal Phenomenon *

Is it possible that the consumers who drop out first as price of a connoisseur good increases are not the same as those who would exit first if quality declined? This problem can once again be analyzed by means of a simple modification of the traditional demand diagram. Suppose there are three buyers, $A$, $B$, $C$, who would be ready to buy one unit of a connoisseur good at prices $P_a$, $P_b$, and $P_c$—their demand is shown by the respective elongated rectangles in figure 4a. Suppose actual unit price is $P$ so that $A$, $B$, and $C$ each buy one unit. $A$ is the person with the highest consumer surplus, followed by $B$ and $C$. If price rises to $P'$ while quality remains unchanged customer $C$ drops out. Now draw a diagram (see 4b) with quality (deterioration) instead of price (increase) measured along the vertical axis and examine what happens if quality deteriorates with price unchanged. Prior to deterioration, quality must have been such, as for example at $Q$, that all three customers bought the good. Now quality worsens to a point, say $Q'$, that one of the three buyers is eliminated. The argument of Chapter 4 indicates that quite conceivably not $C$, but $A$ is going to be the one to withdraw. The reason is that for $A$ the quality drop from $Q$ to $Q'$ is equivalent to an increase in price that wipes out all of his consumer surplus, whereas for $C$ the equivalent price increase may be so small that he remains in the market. The different price equivalents of a quality decline are indicated by the different distances of the dashed line segments from the horizontal line drawn through $P$. As a result of the assumed situation it is clear that the order in which the three consumers are arranged in the quality diagram will be the *reverse* of that in the price diagram: the marginal consumer from the point of view of price has become the most intra-marginal consumer in case of quality deterioration, and vice versa.

This "reversal phenomenon" is of course only one of several possibilities. For a good to qualify as a *connoisseur good*, it is only required (a) for the price increase equivalents into which a quality decline can be translated to be different for different consumers and (b) for these equivalents to be positively cor-

* See text pages 47–50.

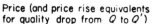
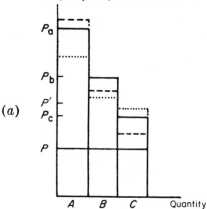

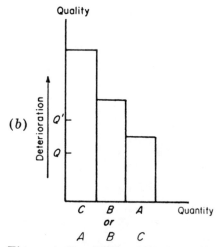

Figure 4. Possibility of the reversal phenomenon in the case of connoisseur goods

related with the corresponding consumer surpluses.[1] These two conditions are compatible with a situation in which $C$, the price-

1. It should be added that this second condition defines a connoisseur good only when consumer incomes are not too dissimilar.

marginal consumer, drops out first also when quality declines while $A$, the most quality-conscious consumer, stays longest in case of a quality drop simply because he has so large a consumer surplus to begin with that even a high price increase equivalent of a given quality decline fails to wipe it out entirely. This possibility is indicated by the dotted lines in the price diagram and their distances from the $P$ price line. In such a situation, the chances for voice to play an important role would be excellent, for the high-consumer-surplus customers are obviously unhappy about the large loss in welfare they are sustaining, but are unable to find a satisfactory alternative. Hence, as long as they continue to buy the good they will wield what influence they have with a view to having its quality improved.

# Appendix D.
## Consumer Reactions to Price Rise and Quality Decline in the Case of Several Connoisseur Goods *

A consumer with a desire for a connoisseur good can choose between the numerous varieties of this good that may be available. He is willing to pay more for higher quality, but obviously within the limits of (a) his budget and (b) his ability to appreciate ever higher quality. Thus for each consumer there exists an indifference map showing the various combinations of price and quality which yield equivalent satisfaction for a *given quantity* (say, one car or one case of champagne) of the good.

Several such indifference curves are shown in figure 5a, in which quality (improvement) is measured along the horizontal and price (increase) along the vertical axis so that any movement in the southeasterly (rather than, as usual, the northeasterly) direction represents here an unambiguous increase in consumer welfare.

The two constraints within which consumers are placed are indicated by the lines marked "quality appreciation ceiling" and "budget ceiling." Even though only one pair of ceilings is shown, they are of course likely to be quite different for different consumers. The quality appreciation ceiling indicates the limit beyond which the consumer is unable to derive any increase in satisfaction from further improvement in quality. Hence he will be unwilling to pay more for higher quality beyond that ceiling. The budget ceiling can be understood as either the total income of the consumer, if there is only one good or, in a world of many goods, as an arbitrary figure which he has set himself, at current prices, as the limit for his spending on the article in question.[1] Indifference curves may hit the

* See text pages 50–54.

1. The number of units of the connoisseur good that are purchased is assumed to remain unchanged when consumers substitute some new variety of the good for the usually bought one as a result of changes in the latter's quality or price. The trade-off explored here is that between different varieties (price-quality combinations) of one unit (or of a fixed number of units) of the good, rather than that between quality and quantity. For analysis of the latter trade-off see H. S. Houthakker, "Compensated Changes in Quantities and

Appendix D

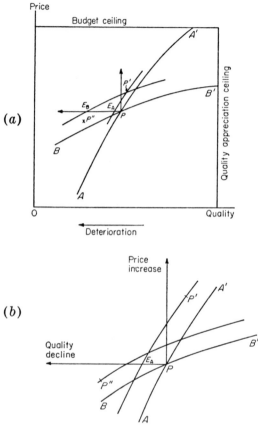

(a)

(b)

Figure 5. Reactions of price-conscious and quality-conscious consumers to price rise and quality decline

budget ceiling before reaching the quality ceiling as in the case of indifference curve *AA'* which is drawn to represent the

Qualities Consumed," *Review of Economic Studies*, 19:155–164 (1952–1953). Although quality is often traded off against quantity in consumer purchases, the situation under discussion is perhaps of greater practical significance. This is so essentially because many important consumer decisions are indivisible, or *are thought of* as indivisible; a consumer is getting *a* dinner, *a* car, *a* house, *an* education for his children, and in his mind he weighs prices of these goods or services against their qualities instead of adjusting quantities bought to quality.

quality-conscious or fastidious consumer who will gladly pay more money for even small quality improvements. Indifference curve *BB'* represents the undiscerning or price-conscious consumer who requires substantial quality improvements if he is to pay a higher price for the article. *BB'* hits the quality appreciation ceiling before the budget ceiling: at that point its slope has become horizontal indicating precisely that a further increase in quality brings no further welfare gain and precludes therefore also the acceptance of a higher price.

The following analysis is carried out on the assumption that both quality-conscious and price-conscious consumers operate at some distance below the two ceilings. In particular, budgets do not set rigid limits to the quality which can be afforded.[2]

The conditions under which consumers shift from one quality-price combination to another in case of quality deterioration or price increase of the usually bought variety can now be examined. Assume first that just two varieties of the connoisseur good are available, one represented by the price-quality combination of point *P*, the other by point *P'* at which both price and quality are *higher*. Later on, another variety represented by point *P''* whose price and quality are both lower than those pertaining to *P* will be considered. The diagram has been so drawn that both consumers will reach their highest indifference curve by buying the variety represented by *P*.[3]

What happens in the course of gradual quality deterioration

2. If quality-price trade-offs are uniform for all consumers, as was approximately the case in the example of tires or railroad services cited in ch. 4 above, then indifference curves will be parallel straight lines of uniform slope. Suppose, to give a more extreme example, that the "quality" difference between two "varieties" of toothpaste comes down to one containing twice the number of ounces of exactly the same compound. Then, except for the intrusion of time preference, storage space, and other factors of comparatively minor importance in this context, the consumer will be indifferent between them provided the larger tube costs twice as much.

3. This is indicated by the fact that the other available varieties, such as *P'* and *P''*, are inferior to both *AA'* and *BB'*. The diagram shows how it is possible for the *same* variety to be bought by both quality- and price-conscious consumers as undoubtedly happens all the time in the market. Only if the array of available varieties were completely continuous, so that the "variety-connecting curve" (see below) is really a curve rather than a limited number of points, would consumers with different tastes concerning price-quality combinations never buy the same variety.

of the normally bought variety? If price remains the same, the quality decline can be shown along the horizontal line leading west from $P$. This line will intersect at $E_A$ (exit A) an indifference curve of the quality-conscious consumer that passes through the other available, higher-quality good $P'$ long before it crosses at $E_B$ a similar indifference curve belonging to the less fastidious consumer. Thus it is clear that whenever the only other available good is of higher quality and price the quality-conscious consumer will exit before the less demanding one. By exactly the same reasoning it could be shown that the converse proposition holds: the less demanding customer exits first when the only available competing variety is of lesser quality and price, shown in the diagram by point $P''$. When both a higher-quality, higher-priced ($P'$) and a lower-quality, lower-price substitute ($P''$) are available, the quality-conscious consumers will exit, in case of deterioration of $P$, toward $P'$ and, some time later in the process of deterioration, the less fastidious consumers will exit toward $P''$.[4]

The reversal phenomenon, namely the tendency of the price-intramarginal consumers to get out first when quality declines, can also be more precisely defined with the help of this diagram. An interesting result is that no reversal takes place when there are only two commodities, either $P$ and $P'$ or $P$ and $P''$. Suppose there is only the former pair. Price increases for variety $P$ can be shown by the vertical line starting at $P$, just as quality declines are shown by the horizontal line. Clearly *both* the vertical and the horizontal lines will cross first the indifference curve of

4. From the point of view of an individual consumer, a good with price and quality both higher than those pertaining to the normally bought variety can in this fashion be converted into a good of equivalent satisfaction which would have the same price as the normally bought variety and a lower quality. This "equivalent variety" is of course different for consumers with different degrees of quality- or price-consciousness. For this reason it was stated that point $Q_E$ in figure 3 could be different for different consumers. Thus, the seemingly restrictive assumption that point $Q_E$ represents a commodity of lower quality and identical price can be dropped without any change in the analysis of the voice-exit choice that was presented. Point $Q_E$ must simply be reinterpreted as the identical-price equivalent, according to an individual consumer's indifference map, of a variety whose quality and price both differ from those of the normally bought one.

the quality-conscious consumer going through $P'$. Hence there is no reversal in this case, although the quality-conscious consumer will exit much more promptly in the case of quality decline than in case of price increase; but he will always be the one to exit first, just as in the opposite case, when only $P$ and $P''$ exist, the less fastidious consumer would always find himself in that role. For the reversal phenomenon to show up, one must specify the simultaneous existence of at least three varieties, $P$, $P'$, and $P''$, *with $P'$ and $P''$ on opposite sides of $P$.* Then, as can be seen in the blown up figure 5b, the price-increase line may cross first the indifference curve of the less demanding consumer going through $P''$ whereas the quality-decline line would pass first through the indifference curve of the more demanding consumer going through $P'$. In other words, when price of the normally bought good increases, the less fastidious consumer exits first (toward $P''$) while the highly quality-conscious consumer exits first when quality declines (toward $P'$). The order in which the two consumers exit is effectively reversed in the case of quality decline in relation to what happens in the case of price increase.

Hence, far from being a *curiosum,* the reversal phenomenon appears to be rather the normal case in competitive markets in which several price-quality combinations are available.

One further note. $P$, $P'$, and $P''$ represent in the diagram the various varieties between which consumers can choose. It is likely that if a "variety-connecting" curve were drawn through $P$, $P'$, and $P''$ it would, like the transformation curve, be convex in the direction opposite to that of the indifference curves, for the reason that it will normally be increasingly expensive to improve quality by "equal" amounts (quality being measured by some "objective" criterion, that is, a criterion other than price itself). It is clear from the diagram that the speed with which the quality-conscious consumers will desert a deteriorating product will depend to a considerable extent on the availability of a close higher-quality substitute. For this reason, the differential *density* with which the variety-connecting curve is actually occupied by distinct varieties in the neighborhood of the particular point under observation has great relevance for appraising the respective roles of exit and voice, as is brought out in Chapter 4.

# Appendix E.
## The Effects of Severity of Initiation
## on Activism: Design for an Experiment *

How members of a group respond to a deterioration in the group's functioning, activities, or output is the central problem of this book which, in this form, has not been directly investigated by social psychologists. A closely related question has, however, received theoretical and experimental attention: it consists in exploring the reactions of various categories of members who find, upon joining a group, that the group's activities are less enjoyable, useful, or profitable than they expected. One of the more interesting, somewhat counter-intuitive derivations from Leon Festinger's *Theory of Cognitive Dissonance* (1957) showed that liking for a group increases with increasing severity of initiation or expense required to join that group; that is, one who has suffered to enter a group will perceive it as more attractive (or as less unattractive) than one who has not. Thus, if the group activities are so arranged as to be "objectively" disappointing, the member who has suffered severe initiation will perceive them as less so than one who has paid a low or no price of entry. This finding is, if not challenged, at least substantially modified by the hypothesis developed in Chapter 7. It is there argued that those who have been severely initiated could under certain circumstances become an active minority which would engage in innovative, reformist, insurgent, or secessionist behavior. Before this hypothesis is spelled out in greater detail, the present state of knowledge in the field will be briefly surveyed.

### The effects of severity of initiation on liking for a group

In all groups there are usually some aspects which an individual does not like. If he has experienced an unpleasant, painful, or otherwise severe initiation, the cognition that he has undergone such an unpleasant ordeal to attain membership is dissonant with the cognitions concerning the undesirable

* See text pages 94–96. This appendix was written by Philip G. Zimbardo and Mark Snyder, in collaboration with the author.

aspects of the group. This dissonance can be reduced in two ways: either by changing the cognition about the unpleasantness of the initiation, that is, by minimizing its perceived unpleasantness; or by changing some or all of the cognitions about the undesirable features of the group, that is, by emphasizing the attractive and ignoring the undesirable aspects of the group. For mildly unpleasant initiations (low dissonance), the first alternative is most likely, but with increasing severity of initiation (higher dissonance), it becomes increasingly difficult to distort the objective facts of the severe, unpleasant, or painful initiation and considerably easier to distort the more subjective perceptions of the group. Thus, as initiation becomes more severe, dissonance increases, and the liking for the group should increase to reduce this dissonance.

To test this derivation, Aronson and Mills [1] assigned female college students who had volunteered to participate in group discussions on sex to either a severe initiation (high dissonance), mild initiation (low dissonance), or a control group (no initiation). Initiation for the severe condition consisted in reading aloud to a male experimenter twelve obscene words and two vivid descriptions of sexual behavior. The mild initiation required reading aloud only five innocuous sex-related words. The control group did not read aloud. All subjects were then informed that they had passed the embarrassment test and could therefore join an in-progress group discussion. In order to provide constant stimulus material, the subject had to listen to the other members, but could not talk, on the pretext that they were discussing a book she had not read. She then heard an extremely trite discussion of secondary sexual activity in lower animals in which the group (four undergraduate girls) droned on, contradicted themselves, and were in general very uninteresting. After this discussion, the subject rated the discussion and the participants. These scale ratings served as dependent measures of attitude toward the group.

The results were clear cut. Coeds who underwent the severe initiation of reading obscene material liked both the group and

1. See ch. 7, n. 10, above.

its members more than either girls who underwent a mild initiation or no initiation at all. The latter two groups did not differ from each other.

The Aronson-Mills experiment and results have been the target of numerous criticisms and alternative explanations. Criticism centered on certain aspects of the procedural operation used to test the conceptual relationships between the severity of initiation and group liking. Both the initiation and the group discussion related to sex; thus, the severe initiation may have sexually aroused the girls making them more anxious to get into the group. Or, the initiation may have set up an expectation that there would be more interesting and sexy discussions in the future. Also, subjects who have succeeded at the severe initiation may feel more reinforced or pleased with their successful performance than those who have passed a mild initiation, and, hence, they may have rated the group as more likeable.

These criticisms may be evaluated by repeating the essence of the Aronson-Mills experiment while eliminating (1) those explanations based on the content of the initiation, through use of an initiation qualitatively different from the nature of the group discussion, and (2) those explanations based on relative success feelings, by withholding feedback as to the subject's success or failure on the initiation task.

Such an experiment was performed by Gerard and Mathewson [2] using physical pain (electric shock) as the initiation, varying presence or absence of test feedback, and including conditions in which subjects were shocked but were not told that this was part of the initiation procedure. The results were very encouraging for the dissonance theory prediction that the more severe the initiation (increased pain) the more the subjects liked the boring group discussion (this time about cheating in college), whether or not they were told they had passed the pain test. In the noninitiation condition (shock only, not described as initiation) no dissonance can be created by the boring nature of the discussion because one has not suffered for the express purpose of achieving membership in that boring group.

2. See ch. 7, n. 10, above.

Hence one would not predict increased liking in this case. The fact that the dissonance predictions are substantiated only when potential dissonance exists (initiation condition only) gives, of course, further support for the dissonance theory explanation of the relationship between severity of initiation and liking for a group. In fact, the results were even stronger than in the original Aronson and Mills experiment.

## The effects of severity of initiation on activism

Both the Aronson-Mills and the Gerard-Mathewson experiments were arranged in such a way that the activities of the group were experienced only once, during a brief session, by the subjects. Moreover, the experimental situation was such that there was no room for any initiative or active participation by the various initiates, severe or mild. Both these conditions are unrealistic. Group activities go on over a long period and members are not just passively experiencing the "goings-on." It is therefore likely that the experiments so far conducted have tested merely the *initial* reaction of severe and mild initiates to an unsatisfactory group. Once these initiates turn into members of an ongoing group, while group activities continue to be disappointing, the cognition to this effect will be less and less amenable to being denied and dismissed. The initial way out of the dissonance is therefore increasingly unavailable, but two other ways of reducing dissonance are opening up and are likely to appeal particularly to those who entered the group with high expectations because of severe initiation: (1) exit from the group and (2) active reorganization and improvement of the group through creative innovation and reformist activities.

The first alternative is only possible when one can easily resign from the group; that is, when the *costs of exit* are low. Moreover, it is not necessarily a satisfactory solution, as it generates further dissonance (between the cognitions "I have suffered, or paid a high entry cost, to join the group" and "now I am leaving the group"). One might expect that to the extent that there are similar groups available (groups, that is, which serve the same functional goals), this switching of allegiance will be more likely. When exit is costly or otherwise difficult, one will probably attempt to reduce the exit-generated dissonance by seeking social support for the action of exiting: in particular, one may try to convince others to do likewise. In other words, the severe initiate will be a critic of the group either from the inside threatening to exit and pressuring others to do so also, or from the outside after exiting.

The second alternative is theoretically and practically the most interesting. When exit is difficult or impossible, an effective way to reduce the dissonance between liking for the group and knowledge of its shortcomings is to take action to reorganize the group and to remove its negative aspects. This solution is beneficial to the individual because it effectively solves his cognitive dilemma. It is of even more value to the group because it improves the group through creative innovation and increases its prospects for long-term viability. The probability that activist behavior and creative innovation will occur in response to the discrepancy between high expectations and the current reality of the negative features of the group is also a function of the various costs the individual is likely to incur in the course of such behavior. For example, he must expend time, effort, personal skills, and other resources, as well as incur the risk of being proved wrong, in case it turns out that the group cannot be changed or that he does not command sufficient influence.

The new hypotheses to be tested can now be briefly stated. Individuals who undergo a severe initiation to become members of a group that turns out to be unsatisfactory will only initially express more liking for this group than do the mild initiates. In time, the severe initiates will take the lead in active innovative behavior to remove sources of dissatisfaction from the group. Behaviorally, this will result in suggesting ways to improve the group, forming committees to devise improvements, seeking out and communicating both with the leaders and other members of the group. Furthermore, severe initiates who exit will actively recruit other members to leave with them and otherwise seek social support.

When taking action either to improve the group or to exit from it, the severe initiates are likely to justify this action to themselves and others by depicting the present state of the group as even more "rotten" than it really is; and they will at that point have a poorer opinion of the group than the mild initiates. Hence, in the course of their experience as group members, the severe initiates should pass from a state of liking the group *more* than the mild initiates to ∴ state in which they like it *less*. It will be interesting to see whether this prediction can be experimentally verified.

## The experiment

The general hypotheses stated above will be tested in an experimental paradigm based on that employed by Aronson and Mills (1959) and Gerard and Mathewson (1966) with the modification that subjects will actually join and participate in several sessions with a group which is thoroughly uninteresting. Subjects will be recruited on a volunteer basis from the Stanford University undergraduate student body to participate in a series of five hypnosis training sessions for which they will be paid $x$ dollars. Subjects will undergo either a severe initiation, mild initiation, or no initiation (control group). They will be led to believe that failure to complete the entire series will result in the loss of the entire $x$ dollars (high cost of exit) or only in loss of payment for missed sessions (low cost of exit). The design is thus a 3 x 2 factorial with severity of initiation and cost of exit as the two factors. The actual experiment will consist of only the initiation procedure and three sessions during which time there will be measures of liking for the group, its activities, and members, as well as various opportunities to demonstrate activist or innovative behavior designed to improve the uninteresting organization and activities of the group.

## Procedure

When subjects who have previously volunteered to participate in a five-session hypnosis training program arrive at the laboratory, they will fill out a biographical questionnaire in which the key items will be reasons for volunteering and measures of expectations about the group, its activities, and its members: 100-point continuous scales measuring liking, interest, dullness,

Appendix E

productivity, educational value, intelligence, entertainment, attraction to the group, organization, and so forth. These same scales will be repeated after each initiation and after each group session as measures of liking and attraction to the group. The comparative base line will be data for a group of subjects who have undergone an interesting series of hypnosis group sessions.

All subjects except the no-initiation controls will then undergo an initiation to the group described as a selection procedure to eliminate those subjects who will not be psychologically or physically capable of being successful hypnotic inductees—or of working well with the others in the group. Subjects then will be assigned at random to either severe-initiation or mild-initiation conditions. Control subjects will bypass this stage of the procedure.

The virtue of using hypnosis training as the major group activity is that initiation severity can be meaningfully introduced as a natural part of the assessment procedure (which was somewhat artificial in both of the prior studies). The severe initiation will consist of a number of activities involving a fairly high degree of physical exertion or discomfort. The mild initiation will consist of qualitatively identical but quantitatively lesser versions of each of these severe initiation activities. All of these will be described to subjects as activities employed in evaluating effects of hypnotic induction on psychological and physiological functioning. After initiation, the subject will be informed of the conditions of payment for participation in the project: either receipt of $x$ dollars at the end *only* if all sessions are attended (high cost of exit manipulation), or loss of $x/5$ dollars for each session not completed (low cost of exit manipulation).

Before entering his group, each subject will read the autobiographical statements of the other subjects, be told he will work with this particular group for the entire time, and then complete a questionnaire measuring his expectancies about the group's sessions to provide measures of expected attraction and liking as a function of severity of initiation. Each subject then will be introduced to the other members of the group. Each group will consist of seven subjects—two severe initiates, two mild initiates, two control subjects, and a confederate of the

152

experimenter ("blind" to the others) whose role will be described below—and a group leader (an experimenter, also "blind").

Session 1: The first session consists of a tape-recorded speech entitled "What is hypnosis?" in which the speaker presents a lengthy collection of utterly trite "little known facts about hypnosis" mainly consisting of trivial information about early hypnotists, and an involved, confusing, and contradictory discussion of appropriate experimental design for evaluating success of hypnotic induction. Subjects are then exposed to a tape-recorded standard hypnotic susceptibility test, which is long and uninteresting. At this point a break is announced, before which subjects are required to rate their attitudes toward the group again.

Session 2: After a ten-minute break, during which subjects are not permitted to discuss the proceedings (but are told to think about what they learned and then complete attention to the group scales), the second session convenes. The tape-recorded susceptibility test from the first session is repeated (for "reliability"), after which the group leader proceeds to "interpret" the test to them. Shortly thereafter, he begins a boring talk about hypnotic susceptibility and the statistically relevant issues. The confederate referred to above now threatens to exit, saying this is not what he volunteered for, and asks how many others will join him in doing so. The experimenter makes it clear that participation is voluntary and only willing subjects can be used, so anyone who wants to leave can do so. The number of subjects agreeing with the confederate is used as a measure of exit, as is of course the number of subjects who might spontaneously express the desire to leave. Subjects who threaten to leave are told that they should stay until the third session is over and just not return the next evening for the last two sessions. This eliminates subject loss problems. We may also note attempts by members to prevent anyone from exiting. At the end of this session, the experimenter distributes the regular questionnaire which once again measures attitude toward the group as well as another questionnaire asking for suggestions to change the organization and activity of the group. This serves as the third measure of creative innovative behavior.

Session 3: After a short break, the third session reconvenes, without the experimenter present. A graduate student enters the room and informs the group that the group leader asked him to terminate this session, give information about the next sessions, and collect some information from them. He reads a statement that the next two sessions will be similar to the last one, and gives out some details about the future sessions. He also reviews each subject's original "commitment-liking" ratings in order to make the dissonance salient—he does so *privately*.

Next, students are told that those wishing to meet with the instructor to discuss the group activities or their participation could see the instructor during his office hours, and should make appointments to do so. Subjects are asked to indicate which issues they intend to discuss, the time they will arrive, and an estimate of the length of time they wish to spend with the group leader. These expressions of intent serve as a "behavioroid" measure of innovative motivation, and the number of subjects who actually keep their appointments serves as a purely behavioral one.

Finally, the graduate student leads a "spontaneous" discussion initiated by the confederate (if no one else does so). It is tape-recorded and coded for creative innovation, suggestions for improving the group, and threats of exit on the part of each subject. The session then ends, with the reminder that the final two sessions are to be held the next two evenings. Those subjects who arrive the next evening are all debriefed, paid for their participation, and then given the opportunity to participate in genuine hypnosis training. Those subjects who do not appear are similarly debriefed, paid, and offered the opportunity for real training, by mail. All subjects receive a full statement of the results of the experiment once it is completed.

## Summary of response measures

The dependent measures in this study are the following:
1. Measures of liking for and attraction to the group
   a. pre-experimental
   b. after initiation
   c. after each session

2. Measures of exit
   a. spontaneous
   b. in response to model's threat of exit
3. Measures of voice and innovation
   a. spontaneous comments
   b. questionnaire suggestions
   c. appointments with group leader
   d. group discussion performance
   e. arrival for appointments, and comments to group leader at that time

## Expected results

1. There will be greater initial liking for the group as severity of initiation is greater.

2. There will be greater initial liking for the group as exit costs are higher.

3. There will be a higher frequency of threats of exit as severity of initiation and exit costs are less—in early stages of dissatisfaction.

4. There will be more exits from the group with minimal initiation severity and exit costs.

5. There will occur a marked temporal change in the attitude toward the group of those subjects who were given the severe initiation (and the high exit costs). There will be little or no criticism at first (in fact, they should initially defend the group against criticism), but at some point, these subjects will become most critical of the group as they orient themselves toward either voice or exit.

6. Any new group action will be generated by subjects given the severe initiation and subjected to the high cost of exit.

7. However, if the subjects are not able to influence the group and actually exit from it, their high level of motivation will be used against the group. They, much more so than the earlier exiting members who were given weak initiation and subjected to low exit costs, will proselytize to actively undermine the group. They ought to seek social support for the exit action, preferably by convincing others to exit.

# Index

Activism, 94; political, 32, 71–72, 74; and severity of initiation, 146–155
Acton, Lord, 116
Almond, Gabriel A., viii, 30n, 32n, 96n
Alternative, availability of, 66–68, 71, 81–82, 145
*American Capitalism* (Galbraith), 57
American Revolution, 106
Anderson, Norman H., 91n
Apathy, political, 32
Apter, David, 97n
Aronson, E., 94n–95n, 147–149, 151
Arrow, Kenneth, 18–19
Ayres, R. E., 73n

Baboons, 5–6
Ball, George, 115n, 118n
Banfield, Edward, 39
Baran, Paul, 13n
Becker, Gary, 11
Behavior: lapses in, 1–2; loyalist, 86–98
*Behavioral Theory of the Firm, The* (Cyert and March), 11
Bergson, Abram, viii
Bickel, Alexander M., 85
Black power, vii, 109, 112
Bloch-Lainé, François, 58n
Bolivia, 110
Bonini, Charles P., 13n
Bowen, W. G., 73n
Boycott, 86
"Brain drain," 81
Brazil, Northeast, 111
Britain, 11–12, 118
Bunzel, John H., 109n
Bureaucracy, *see* Government
Business firms, *see* Firms

Carmichael, Stokely, 109n

Center for Advanced Study in the Behavioral Sciences, vii, viii, 5
Chamberlain, Neville, 118
Cheng, Hing Yong, 58n
Church, 33, 76, 96
CIO-AFL, 28–29; No-Raiding Agreement, 29
Clark, John Maurice, 22n
Clausen, A. R., 71n
Coercion, 97n
Cognitive dissonance, 94–96, 147–149; modification of theory of, 93–96, 113–114, 146, 149–155
Colombia, 61
Competition, vii, 2–3, 9, 21–22, 55–61; monopolistic, 2; "normal," 21; as recuperation mechanism, 25; as collusive behavior, 26–29, 124; and monopoly's efficiency, 58–59; in American ideology, 112
Congress party, India, 84
Connoisseur goods, 49–51, 138–140; defined, 138; and price rise and quality decline, 141–145
Consumer durable goods, 41–42
*Consumer Reports,* 25
Consumer research organizations, 42
"Consumer revolution," 42. *See also* Nader, Ralph
Consumer surplus, 48–50, 138–141
Consumers, 21, 125; and cost of voice option, 40; channels of communication for, 42–43; quality conscious, 50–52, 79, 96; sensitivity to quality change, 62; "captive," 70–75
Converse, P. E., 71n
Cooper, Duff, 118

**157**

Index

**161**

Index